The Eleventh Hour

The Eleventh Hour

General Lewis W. Walt, USMC (Ret.)

Foreword by
Eugene V. Rostow

Caroline House Publishers, Inc.
Ottawa, Illinois & Thornwood, New York

ISBN = 0-89803-005-6 (clothbound)
ISBN = 0-89803-025-0 (paperbound)
Library of Congress Catalogue Card Number: 79-83563
Manufactured in the United States of America

To all those Americans who have sacrificed their lives
on the field of battle in the defense of our liberties

ACKNOWLEDGEMENTS

I would like to express my deep appreciation to Mr. Charles Reese and Mr. Jack Peterson for their expert assistance in writing this book, and to my wife, June, for her patience and encouragement.

CONTENTS

ix

Preface

This book is addressed primarily to the twenty-nine million Americans who have served their country in the Armed Forces and to those millions of young Americans who will have to bear the burdens of future wars. It is a call to arms, a plea to all of you to fight a battle now to prevent a war tomorrow. Unless you respond—both veteran and youth—the sacrifices of the past and the promises of the future will vanish down the drain of history.

I have never asked Marines to go into battle without telling them exactly what they faced so far as I knew it. My one unbreakable rule has always been to stick with facts and tell the truth. That is what I am going to do in this book.

The facts are these: the United States has been brought, by its own civilian leaders, to a position of military inferiority to the Soviet Union. At this moment, you and your loved ones stand exposed to physical destruction. The option of whether you shall live or die rests primarily with the hardened men who occupy the Kremlin. If they should choose tomorrow or next year or the year after to annihilate you and your family, there is little the U.S. government could do to stop them except to surrender.

No generation of Americans has ever before been so recklessly placed at the mercy of so pitiless and powerful an enemy. What's worse is that at this moment of greatest danger the men who are responsible for having placed us in the kill zone are still calling the shots in Washington.

There are no incoming missiles in our skies because the Soviet leaders believe that with patience they can in a short time force us to surrender. I am not talking about some date in the far distant future, but some day within the next four or five years. Their ultimatum, when it comes, will place on the shoulders of our leaders the terrible decision to fight a thermonuclear war we cannot win or to hand over the American people to an oligarchy of tyrants whose viciousness and brutality have no match in the long, bloody history of man's cruelty. As Ernest Hemingway wrote at the beginning of World War II, there are several things worse than war and they all come with defeat.

For thirty-four years I proudly wore the uniform of the Marine Corps. I fought the Japanese, the North Koreans, the Chinese, the North Vietnamese and the Viet Cong with every ounce of energy God gave me. For thirty-four years mine was a world of war and arms, of command and obedience, of unquestioned loyalty, and support of the Constitution. Politics was foreign to that world.

But I have learned as well as bled. I have learned that the successes bought at such dear prices in lives on the battlefields are made necessary by the failures in the political arena at home. I have learned that wrong thinking, carelessness, greed and apathy kill and maim, too. I am asking you to combat these weaknesses in our politics lest they once more unleash the dogs of war.

Our loyalty to the Constitution must remain firm, but we must battle in the political arena with the same unity, the same ferocity, and the same determination which has carried us to victory on the battlefield. I am asking you, not to destroy but to build, not to kill but to preserve life, not to enslave but to maintain freedom. I am asking that your actions be motivated, not by hatred, but by love for all the good things in this world which must be saved from harm.

I cannot lead you in this battle. The accumulated years are too many, and I have no expertise in this kind of combat. There are younger men, perhaps you, who have the energy and the knowledge to assume command.

What I can do I will do. I can lay out the danger, identify the enemy, and suggest a plan of action which each of you can follow. The objectives are these: 1. to purge the Congress of the forces of appeasement and surrender which are pulling us toward war or slavery; and 2. replace them with men and women of integrity and common sense who will restore our military superiority, the only coin with which we can buy the time for diplomacy to work.

The destiny of the American people belongs in our hands, not in the hands of foreign tyrants. Will you join me in the fight to return it to our shores?

GEN. LEWIS WALT, USMC

Foreword

General Lewis Walt has earned the right to be heard by the American people. His record includes equally distinguished service in the field and in the realm of strategic planning. He thoroughly understands the military element in history, and the relationship between strategic and tactical military power. His protest against the strange decline in our military power during the last decade—a decline which has occurred in the face of a startling and continuing Soviet buildup—is a call for action while there is still time for wise action to prevent war, and consolidate peace.

The immediate problem on which he focuses is the restoration of the clear and visible second strike strategic capacity of the United States—the key to every other aspect of our foreign and defense policy. Our ability to reestablish our second strike capacity can be frustrated by the SALT II agreement now in prospect. This must not be allowed to happen.

The subject of nuclear arms, strategic or tactical, is inherently repulsive, and raises difficult moral issues. We should all agree,

I am sure, that it would be better to have a Treaty abolishing nuclear arms than one which aims only to limit them. In that connection, it is important to mention an episode every American should recall with pride and which General Walt alludes to: the 1947 offer of the Baruch Plan, which had been prepared by Dean Acheson and David Lilienthal. At that time, we had a monopoly of nuclear weapons. If we had wished to do so, we could have commanded the whole world to do our bidding. Instead, we offered to put our nuclear weapons and all we knew about nuclear science into the hands of an international agency, which would have developed nuclear energy for peaceful uses. The Soviet rejection of the Baruch Plan, along with its rejection of the Marshall Plan at about the same time, was a dismal turning point in the history of the Cold War, a signal that the Soviet Union would embark on an imperial course, rather than continue our World War II alliance through programs of peaceful postwar cooperation.

The proposal of the Baruch Plan was a singular event—bold, creative, and idealistic. I venture to predict that when the nations are tired of war and the risk of war again; bored with Empire; and exhausted by the intricacies and uncertainties of nuclear calculations, they will return to the simple ideas of the Baruch Plan. I hope so.

Meanwhile, because of the Soviet decision, we have no choice but to maintain a deterrent nuclear capability, and to keep alive the hope of better days to come.

For nearly a century, there has been a current of opinion in Great Britain, the United States, and the English-speaking countries, committed to the belief that arms limitation agreements are an important instrument of peace. The faith is shared in Scandinavia and the Netherlands, and it is tenaciously held, resisting the challenge of contrary experience.

Thus the arguments made for SALT today are exactly the same as those put forward in behalf of the Washington Naval Treaty of 1922 and the other arms limitation and arms reduction arrangements to which the Western governments devoted so much time, attention, and hope during the twenties.

The Washington Naval Treaty and its progeny led straight to

Pearl Harbor. We, the British, and the French, lulled by the Treaty, and hard pressed in any event to find money for naval building programs, let our navies slide. We did not build our full quotas, or modernize our ships. The Japanese and later the Germans, on the other hand, took full advantage of their quotas.

The post-World War I arms limitation agreements—demilitarization of the Rhineland and the various naval agreements—failed to prevent World War II. I should go further. I conclude that those agreements helped to bring on World War II by reinforcing the blind and wilful optimism of the West, thus inhibiting the possibility of military preparedness and diplomatic actions that could have deterred the war.

Despite this melancholy history, we are told everywhere that the SALT II Treaty will be "politically stabilizing;" and that the breakdown of the SALT negotiations or the rejection of the Treaty by the Senate, would "end detente," "bring back the Cold War," increase the risk of nuclear and of conventional war and revive "the arms race" which would cost us another $20, $70 or $100 billion.

These plausible and popular assertions, which tap the deepest and most generous instincts of the American people, are entirely without substance.

The fact is, as General Walt makes clear, the Cold War is not over. On the contrary, it is worse than it has ever been, featured by Soviet threats and thrusts on a far larger scale than those of the simple days of the Berlin Airlift and the crisis in Greece.

General Walt has performed another service in putting to rest some of the myths generated by the Orwellian language of President Nixon, the principal one being that confrontation has been replaced by negotiation in our relationship with the Soviet Union.

The Soviet Union *is* engaged in a policy of imperial expansion all over the world, despite the supposedly benign influence of SALT I, and its various commitments of cooperation to President Nixon in the name of "detente." The Soviet Union is pursuing that course with accelerating momentum. That momentum—we saw its most recent manifestations in Yemen and Afghanistan—results from two related forces: the startling buildup

xvii

of Soviet strategic and conventional forces during the last sixteen years, and the paralyzing impact on American politics of our collapse in Vietnam.

Again, General Walt has done an excellent job in documenting this buildup.

I agree with General Walt that there is still time to head off the collision between the United States and the Soviet Union foreshadowed by these trends. Moderate rearmament, coupled with a vigorous and active diplomacy of solidarity with our allies and with China, could stabilize world politics by containing the Soviet drive for hegemony. But that goal cannot be achieved unless we participate as leader of the effort. Our nuclear arsenal is the indispensable foundation for any such program.

There can be no question that since Vietnam our nuclear position has slipped from stalemate to the borders of inferiority. While the experts argue about whether we are already inferior to the Soviet Union in overall nuclear power, they are agreed that if present trends continue we shall be significantly inferior—and soon.

If such a situation is allowed to develop, our foreign policy and conventional forces would be impotent, and we would acquiesce. It is the first objective of Soviet policy to achieve such a situation. Soviet leaders believe it would enable them to determine the future course of world politics.

The kind of SALT agreement the Administration is so frantically trying to sell the country is not a step toward detente or toward peace, but an act of appeasement which can only invite more Soviet pressure and more risk. It would freeze us in a position of inferiority, deny us the opportunity to redress the balance, weaken our alliances, and isolate us.

It would be a step toward war, not peace.

As the Committee on the Present Danger, of which I am an officer, has made clear, the present debate over SALT II and the philosophy of appeasement which the Treaty represents is the most critical in modern history for quite literally the survival of the United States and of the West may depend on the outcome.

That is why I am honored to recommend *The Eleventh Hour* to the American people. It is a calm, reasoned and realistic appraisal of our strategic situation by an American who has not only distinguished himself in war, but who has also earned equal distinction for his unquestioned honesty and his sincere desire for peace.

Even though he has as much combat experience as any living Marine, General Walt may have made his greatest contribution to his nation's survival by writing this book.

EUGENE V. ROSTOW
New Haven, Connecticut
January, 1979

Chapter I

Our Crumbling Defenses

On August 6, 1945, a single bomb fell from the belly of a B-29 in the sky over Hiroshima, Japan. From ground zero there rose first a huge fireball and then an ugly and lethal mushroom-shaped cloud which roiled up into the atmosphere. Beneath it, 92,000 people lay dead. Thousands more were dying from radiation and burns. Three days later, the horror was repeated in Nagasaki. What we call World War II was ended.

To me, bone tired and aching with malaria, the nightmares of the Battle of Pelelieu Island still vivid, it was the ending that mattered most at that time. Like millions of Americans in uniform, I could—for the first time in four years—reasonably expect to be alive the next Christmas. It was the end of living with uncertainty, fear, fatigue, filth, and death. I, like everybody else, felt a tremendous soaring of the spirit, a sense of jubilation. We had clawed our way through a dank and foul jungle and finally emerged—alive—on a breeze-swept shore where stretched out before us was the clean, cool sea of peace.

Only in recent years have I come to realize how cruel an illusion that vision of peace was. I can now see with the clarity of hindsight and experience that the dropping of the atomic bomb on Hiroshima was not an end, but a beginning, and that what began was not peace, but a new phase of a larger war in which World War II was only an early battle.

This larger war is now approaching a climax. I'm not sure what future historians will call this war, but I do know they will look back on the years from 1939 to beyond today as a time of one long struggle to the death between freedom and human slavery. This war has been fought not only with arms in Korea, Vietnam, Laos, Cambodia, China, the Middle East, Cuba, Latin America, Eastern Europe and Africa, but inside the United States with words and ideas, with riots and drugs, with treachery and corruption.

And all of it—the battles outside and inside the United States—have been fought with one purpose: to bleed us, to divide us, to confuse us, to weaken us until like a battered prize fighter who can no longer hold his arms up, we stand in a daze and helplessly await the knockout.

The enemies who have been pounding us are the leaders of the Soviet Union and Communist China. They've had a falling out, like two Mafia families competing for the same territory, but neither nation has wavered in its intention to destroy us.

It's late in the fight but for some reason our chief opponent, the Soviet Union, hesitates. I suspect the reason is the growing unrest behind the iron curtain. Brave men and women in Poland, Czechoslovakia, Hungary, the Ukraine, Latvia, Lithuania, and in Moscow are buying us time at terrible personal cost by unnerving the Kremlin bosses with persistent protests against their abuses of human rights.

There's still time, with God's help, to clear our minds and block that knockout punch—to prevent a thermonuclear war. Whether we can or not depends on you, the plain American. I use the words ''plain American'' deliberately. The experts have proven unable to cope with the enemy. If our country is to survive beyond the next five years, it will be due to the efforts of the same plain Americans who so magnificently accepted the challenges of World War II, Korea, and Vietnam. Nobody can denigrate American youth in my presence because I've seen three generations tested by fire and each in turn triumphed.

Our first step must be to assess our situation and I will be blunt: it's grim. You have, if you are like most of us, lived most of your life with the comfortable knowledge that America is the world's most powerful nation in military and economic terms. For most of this century, even in the worst of times, we have never had to live with the fears of military defeat and the brutality of conquerors.

We do now.

If someone in the Kremlin decided at this moment to push the nuclear button, there is nothing your government could do to save the lives of you and your loved ones. Within fifteen to thirty minutes, thermonuclear warheads thousands of times more powerful than the bomb that ruined Hiroshima would be raining down on our Minuteman Missile sites, our strategic bomber bases, and on our cities. The lucky would be incinerated in the fireballs the diameters of which would be measured in miles, or in the fire storms which would roll across the states. Within a matter of hours, somewhere between sixty million and a hundred million men, women, and children would die. The unlucky would be left to seek some bare existence in a poisoned and desolate landscape in which few traces of civilization would remain. The United States would be finished as a nation forever.

This is an ugly fact. The ordinary American does not like to think about it, but avoiding this nightmarish calamity has been the chief occupation of our defense forces for the past thirty-two years. It's what happened to those defense forces in the last eighteen years that prompts me to write this book. As you know, today the U.S. has no civil defense program, no anti-ballistic missiles, and no appreciable defense against even a bomber attack. Our fighter-interceptors have been reduced to about 324 aircraft. Most of the air defense radars have been dismantled or converted to civilian use.

This stripping of our defensive forces has been a deliberate policy move on the part of our civilian defense officials. They believe that by baring our population to the Soviet sword we demonstrate our peaceful intentions. The error in their thinking was to believe that the Soviet Union would follow our example. The

Soviets have reacted in an ominously opposite manner. While we cut back, they built, until today they have the world's most extensive air defense and civil defense systems.

The significance of their defensive efforts lies in this simple proposition: If they can minimize the damage we can do to them, then the threat or reality of a nuclear attack becomes the ultimate weapon to blackmail us, to bring us to our knees. It is my opinion, and the opinion of many others who have studied the military situation, that the Soviets have achieved this ability and nuclear attack has become a viable option.

If the Soviet Union launched a nuclear attack on us, we would lose nearly half our population and most of our industrial capacity. In contrast, the Soviets would probably lose no more than twelve million people. Much of their industrial base would survive. Virtually all of their second strike nuclear and conventional military forces would survive. In short, the Soviet Union could emerge from a nuclear exchange as a still powerful nation, more than capable of dealing with Red China or the puny nuclear forces of France and Great Britain, assuming any of those three had a stomach for war.

In considering if twelve million people would be an acceptable loss, you have to keep in mind that the Soviet leaders have an entirely different attitude toward human life from ours. In World War II, they spent lives profligately, losing twenty million people. They have executed an estimated twenty to forty million of their own people. In the Ukraine alone, they murdered over seven million with forced famine and one of the men who played a key role in that act of genocide was Leonid Brezhnev, the present Soviet dictator.

If you are shocked about our weakness, don't blame yourself. This tragic and dangerous state of unbalance has been kept from the American people. The national news media have refused to consider it news. The political leaders whose folly or apathy created the danger have engaged in a deliberate effort to disguise the true situation. Your military leaders have been silenced by orders from their civilian superiors. Those who have retired to speak out have been stone-walled by the press and ridiculed by the politicians and academic strategists.

This calculated act of unilateral disarmament in the face of a hostile and powerful enemy is one of the most irresponsible acts of government in the history of mankind. Who did it and why will be discussed later, but now you must be given the facts that have been denied you on the evening television news and in the pages of your newspapers.

The concept of deterrence is simple. As developed in the 1950s in response to the acquisition of thermonuclear weapons by the Soviet Union, the idea was simply to construct three separate weapons systems which could survive a surprise nuclear attack and destroy the Soviet Union. So long as this was a reality—and perceived as such by Soviet leaders—there would be no nuclear war. No sane Soviet leader would start one since to do so would be to commit national suicide. We, on moral grounds, would not again be the ones who initiated the use of nuclear weapons.

The Kremlin tested our morality, first in Berlin in 1948 and again in Korea in 1951. They learned in both instances that even though we held a virtual nuclear monopoly and even though our vital interests were threatened, we would suffer thousands of American casualties and still not resort to nuclear war.

Those guilt-ridden Americans who accuse their own nation of warmongering and imperialism conveniently forget that when we had the power to destroy the Soviet Union at virtually no cost to ourselves or to use nuclear blackmail to dictate to the rest of the world, we did neither.

The triad of weapons which provided us with a shield against both nuclear war and nuclear blackmail was based on land-based missiles, submarine-launched missiles, and strategic bombers. These weapons were deployed in such overwhelming numbers compared to Soviet forces that in 1962, when they attempted to introduce nukes into Cuba, President John Kennedy could force them to back down. They had no choice. They had tested us again, perhaps encouraged by what they viewed as our timid foreign policy, but they discovered that the young president, despite his desire for peace, was willing to draw the line.

But since 1963, we have lost more than a valiant president. We have lost the shield as well. Here, in plain language, is the sinister story.

Let's take the bombers. There are still flying only about 316 B-52s. The newest of these is fifteen years old while the oldest is twenty years. That's old for an airplane. The B-52 is slow. Soviet surface to air (SAM) missiles shot them out of the sky over North Vietnam. Soviet fighters have the speed to overtake them from the rear.

In the event of a Soviet first strike, whatever number of those 316 planes which survived and started toward the Soviet Union would face these obstacles: 12,064 SAMs and 2,600 fighter-interceptors guided and directed by 6,500 aerospace defense radars. You don't have to be an expert to see that no matter how resourceful the pilots, not many of these aging planes would make it to their targets.

Your military leaders asked for the B-1, a modern bomber which could compete in air speed against the fighter-interceptors and which could fly at tree-top level to evade those radars and SAMs. But the president and a majority of congress said, "No."

The second leg of the triad is our land-based missile system composed of Minuteman and Titan missiles. There are 1,054 of these silos located in the United States. These fixed sites are known to the Soviet Union. They have had years to pinpoint their locations. The Soviets have deployed 1,477 ICBMs and have developed warheads large enough to destroy our missiles in their silos. Some of these are capable of delivering the equivalent of twenty-five million tons of TNT per missile. For some years, the Soviets had problems with accuracy, but then the U.S. State Department okayed the sale of precision ball bearing technology, which solved that problem! These powerful and now accurate missiles are rolling off Soviet assembly lines at this moment.

Since our Minuteman and Titan missiles are in fixed positions and since we are committed to allowing the Soviets a first strike, there's little doubt that a first salvo would destroy a large percentage of our missiles before they could be fired.

Your military leaders have asked for a mobile missile system to make it impossible for the Soviets to destroy our land-based missiles with a first strike. The president and the congress have delayed and delayed and delayed this project.

The third leg of the triad is our fleet of forty-one ballistic missile submarines. Dr. Henry Kissinger, President Nixon's national security adviser, agreed in an arms limitation pact to freeze our fleet at forty-one with 656 missiles. The Soviets, he agreed, could have sixty-two missile-firing subs. They have built eighty-two which carry 909 missiles.

This is a fine weapons system, probably the best at the moment, but like any other weapons system, it has its limitations. The missiles fired from these submarines have a relatively low yield and are less accurate than land-based missiles. That means they cannot be targeted against the Soviets' reinforced military targets. They are aimed primarily at Soviet cities. Their range is 2,800 miles which means they must maneuver in the open sea. Some new Soviet missiles have a range of 4,200 miles. They can be launched from the Soviet Union's protected waters and reach nearly every important target in the United States.

Furthermore, once we leave the make-believe world of war rooms, diplomatic offices, and academic classrooms and enter the real world of seawater and steel, we have to face the fact that at any given time no more than half of our submarines are on battle stations. The others are in port, vulnerable to first strikes, while those at sea, you can be sure, are tracked by Soviet killer subs. How effectively we don't know.

The point I wish to impress on you is that when you begin to think of strategic deterrence, you have to realize that numbers on paper do not fight wars or deter aggression. Only what is still capable of firing after absorbing a first strike counts. That's why statements like, "Both sides have enough to kill each other seven times over" are not only false but misleading.

Air Force Gen. Nathan Twining, one of the pioneers in the missile age, said it best: "Forces which can't win won't deter." And at this moment, our forces can't win, but those of the Soviet Union can.

To sum up, our strategic triad has aged and lost its ability to deter war. The president and a majority in congress have refused to replace the B-52, designed in 1948; they have delayed building a mobile missile system; they have scrapped our air defense and civil defense; they have delayed the neutron warhead; and they have frozen the third leg of the triad, the nuclear subs, by diplomatic agreement.

Instead of telling the American people in plain language what they have done, as I just did, they have instead confused the American people with talk of detente.

Detente was and is exactly what the Soviet leaders told their own people it is: a psychological ploy to disarm us. All the tremendous advances in armaments the Soviets have made, have been made since the beginning of and during detente. While talking detente, they have been building up a war machine at a faster rate than did Adolph Hitler, who incidentally also spoke of Nazi Germany's desire for peace while he prepared for war.

Ralph Waldo Emerson's observation that he can't hear what you say, because what you *are* thunders so loud, is certainly true of the Soviet Union. Their actions drown out their words—at least those words intended for western ears. If we look, however, at their words intended for Soviet ears, their purposes and intentions are crystal clear.

The evidence from published Soviet military journals, from speeches made within the Communist bloc, and from information obtained from Soviet citizens who have defected to the West is overwhelming and irrefutable that their intentions dovetail perfectly with their growing offensive capabilities.

Soviet military doctrine since the end of World War II has been based on the premise that a nuclear war is not unthinkable, as our civilian strategists believe, but probable and winnable. A part of that doctrine includes belief in the necessity of a preemptive first strike. Their actions—concentration on heavy missiles, antisatellite weapons, strong air and civil defense—are in perfect alignment with a first strike doctrine.

Soviet ideology is also unchanged. They view the world in terms of conflict between their system and our system and they view negotiations, treaties, propaganda, subversion, terrorism, espionage, and alliances as effective weapons in the war against capitalism. Not only is the present Soviet military buildup consistent with its ideology and military doctrine, it is consistent with Russian history, which has often involved imperialistic expansion and hostility toward the West.

Alexander Solzhenitsyn, the great Russian writer who now lives in Vermont, said recently that the momentum toward war within the Soviet Union is so great that he would not be surprised to see the West fall on "any morning."

Early in 1973 Brezhnev, in a speech to East European Communist Party leaders in Prague, Czechoslovakia, said that by 1985 the Soviet Union would be militarily and economically strong enough to exert its will anywhere in the world. Many believe that deadline has since been revised to 1982.

East German Army General Heinz Hoffman, in December, 1975, made a speech in East Berlin in which he declared that a nuclear war against aggressive imperialism would be a just war and that the last phase of capitalism will come when it is destroyed—in a nuclear war.

Consistent with their military doctrine that a nuclear war must be fought with combined arms, the Soviet Union has amassed in Eastern Europe the greatest striking force of conventional arms the world has ever seen. I had an opportunity to see some of these weapons captured by the Israelis. The Soviets have gone to the additional expense of sealing and installing air filters in both tanks and armored personnel carriers to minimize the effects of radiation and chemical warfare gases. It was to counter this threat that your military leaders asked for the neutron bomb. This, too, has been denied. And the date for the final delivery of the last of the Warsaw Pact's most modern weapons? 1982.

As you can see, the military situation is indeed grim. We have allowed our strategic and conventional forces to so deteriorate that chemical and nuclear war, and nuclear blackmail have become viable options in Soviet thinking. The weapons and the manpower needed to restore military balance have been denied us by the politicians. Information about the situation has been denied us by most of the major news media. The advice of military leaders who have spent a lifetime of study and thought has been rejected out of hand by civilians whose arrogance and conceit are exceeded only by their inexperience and lack of practical knowledge.

In the face of overwhelming evidence, these civilians persist in defending their delusion that the road to peace lies with appeasement. I was a young lieutenant in the late 1930s, but I remember the preachers of appeasement who ruled Great Britain and France and brought them both to the brink of destruction with their foolish policies.

Is history repeating itself? Not long after Dr. Kissinger had concluded the Salt I negotiations which conceded the Soviets an advantage in nuclear subs, a friend of mine met the secretary in a hallway.

"Henry, why in God's name did you give them sixty-two subs?" he asked.

"But they wanted ninety-two—I talked them out of thirty," he said.

Such is the triumph of our diplomacy. We will return to these apostles of appeasement in a later chapter but there is more bad news to be faced first. We have not only weakened our defenses to the point of peril, we have in the process become vulnerable to the slower but equally fatal tactic of economic strangulation. It may be that history will not repeat itself precisely, that our world may end, as the poet T. S. Eliot wrote, "Not with a bang, but a whimper."

Chapter II

Weak Arms and Cannonfodder

It is late August. In the vast forests of eastern Russia, crews quickly and methodically ready fifty mobile intermediate range missiles for firing. On the plains of Prussia, the Warsaw Pact armies are rolling through maneuvers. Suddenly, without warming, nuclear-tipped missiles explode on NATO headquarters, on NATO airfields, storage depots and military bases. Spearheaded by Soviet and East German divisions, the Warsaw Army crosses the border and begins a blitzkrieg attack on Western Europe.

The Soviet divisions blast opposing armies with nuclear weapons and roll forward under a screen of smoke and deadly nerve gas. Their tanks and armored personnel carriers are sealed with lead liners to protect the men from radiation, and the special air filtration systems protect the men from the nerve gas. The armored personnel carriers are designed so that the Soviet and East German soldiers can fire their weapons without leaving their protected environments.

As the attack proceeds, 200,000 American dependents frantically try to escape the battle areas, but those who survive are quickly rounded up and become prisoners.

In Washington, a stunned and dismayed American president watches from the War Room as the NATO armies disintegrate. France and Holland surrender. There are riots in England as thousands of leftists demand that Great Britain declare its neutrality in violation of the NATO Treaty.

American soldiers—those who did not desert in a vain effort to save their wives and children—fight valiantly with the West Germans, but they are outgunned and outnumbered. Protective clothing and gas masks are not immediately available and many lives are lost before they are gotten into the hands of the troops. Their tanks are not equipped to fight on a chemically-contaminated battlefield.

For the first time, American soldiers are fighting without air superiority. The Soviet missile attacks on NATO bases combined with their rolling anti-aircraft weaponry and their superior numbers of tactical planes have driven the Allied Air Forces from the skies.

The American laser-guided weaponry goes blind in the smoke. Shortages of ammunition and spare parts develop. Because of the confusion in the European capitals, the president still has not gotten clearance from our allies to unlock our nuclear weapons, though many in the field believe it is now a moot point with so many nuclear depots under attack or destroyed.

The president has been on the hot line with the Soviet Union, but the Soviet response has been hard and unyielding—in fact, it's an ultimatum. The Soviet Union will occupy Western Europe and if the Americans attack the Soviet Union, a nuclear holocaust will be unleashed that will wipe the United States off the face of the earth. Then the president learns that American satellites have been destroyed. Suddenly, the United States is blind.

Meanwhile, the American Navy is trying to assemble enough ships for a convoy. The U.S. merchant fleet has too few ships. The Navy's own fleet of ships, numbering 453, is facing 1,400 Soviet naval vessels. Soviet superiority in submarines and cruise missile technology begins to tell. The first convoy is destroyed. Our anti-submarine forces are depleted.

The scenario I have just outlined is based on facts and real capabilities. The Soviets *do* have a mobile intermediate range

missile deployed and they are easily concealed from satellite re-
connaisance. The Soviets *do* have the capability of destroying
those satellites and thus blinding us and disrupting our commu-
nications.

The Soviet equipment *is* designed and built to fight on a battlefield that is contaminated with nuclear, chemical, and even biological agents. I have had an opportunity to examine some of this
equipment which was captured from Arab armies by the Israelis
in the Yom Kippur War. It is good equipment, well-built and
well-designed and in most cases, superior to NATO's.

In addition to the sealers and special air filtration equipment,
every soldier in the Soviet Army is issued protective clothing and
a gas mask, and trained to fight under these conditions. Each
Soviet division contains mobile wash-down equipment and even
mobile, armored medical units.

The Soviet and Warsaw Pact nations *are* trained and equipped
to follow the doctrine developed by Soviet strategists which calls
for sustained, round-the-clock offensive fighting for a period of
several days—tactics which the NATO forces are not equipped or
trained to cope with.

There *is* a huge imbalance in the conventional forces. The Soviet Union has 50,000 tanks compared to 10,000 for the U.S.
They have 55,000 armored personnel carriers while we have
22,000: they have 20,000 artillery pieces to our 5,000; and 7,000
heavy mortars to our 3,000.

The Soviets *have* achieved air superiority over the U.S. forces
in Europe. On March 6, 1978, Gen. Robert J. Dixon, who was
then chief of the Air Force's Tactical Air Command, was asked
by a U.S. Senate committee if the American Air Force could
succeed against the Soviet Air Force. His answer was a flat "No."

The Soviets *have* developed both the tactics, the training, and
the equipment to fight a continuous, round-the-clock offensive for
a number of days—a fact some of our generals refuse to face, just
as some of our generals in other decades refused to face the fact
that an airplane could sink a battleship or that armor and infantry
fighting together could chew up infantry fighting alone.

It is quite possible for the Warsaw Pact armies to launch an attack under the guise of maneuvers. Our diplomats tried to include in the Helsinki Agreement a clause which stipulated that both sides would give advance notice of any large scale maneuvers. The Soviets agreed but left themselves a large loophole.

We do have 200,000 American dependents in the forward areas of Europe and many American officers believe a sizable number of our soldiers would desert in an attempt to save the lives of their wives and children.

Removing the dependents will mean we will have to rotate our troops more often, but given our present knowledge of Soviet capabilities, it is gross negligence to leave women and children in the forward areas where they will almost surely become casualties or hostages.

Rep. Robin Beard, R-Tenn., conducted a detailed study of the volunteer army in 1978 and some of his findings confirmed what I had learned from talking to officers and enlisted men. Our soldiers in Europe are worried and their morale is low. They are worried about their families. They are worried about equipment and ammunition shortages. They are worried about the inadequacy of the M-16 rifle against the Russian AK-47. They are worried about lack of training and about the quality of soldier that the volunteer concept is producing.

Ammunition, spare parts, and replacement equipment reserves are low. In an effort to rebuild these reserves, the Army had announced its intentions to take equipment from divisions based in the U.S. This is a case of tragic shortsightedness, because those divisions will be needed for reinforcements if there is war.

What your military leaders have been forced to do in recent years is to accept politically-imposed budget limitations and then try to devise a strategy which will cope, within that budget. What they should be doing, of course, is devising a strategy that will cope with the real threat and budgeting for it.

Much of the trouble began with the decision to eliminate the draft and rely on an all-volunteer army. It was a politically popular decision, but it was a wrong decision. It has caused a tremendous escalation in the costs of recruitment and personnel. Personnel costs now consume nearly 60 cents of every defense dollar compared to 25 cents for the Soviets.

This means that for every $1 appropriated, we have only 40 cents with which to buy research, fuel, weapons, ammunition, and training supplies. When you factor in the inflation rate, you can readily see that we are not getting much bang for our bucks.

This terrible shortage of dollars is resulting in less training. In the past, one of the excuses used for the imbalance in arms was that our people were allegedly better trained than the Soviets. So, assuming that was true, we have destroyed one more advantage by cutting back so heavily on training.

In Congressman Beard's study, in which his staff interviewed nearly 1,000 people from privates to field grade officers, there was a consistent theme expressed by all the enlisted personnel: they were not satisfied with their training. They wanted more and better training.

In the air-conditioned rooms of the Pentagon, in the White House and in the Congress, you can look at reports and indulge in make-believe and rationalization. But when you are a young soldier in the fields of West Germany staring down the muzzles of the Warsaw Pact guns, you know how well trained you and your comrades are, you know what the situation is in terms of weapons and ammunition supply, and you know how small your chances for survival are.

It is so bad that some of these young men, junior officers and noncommissioned officers, volunteered to appear before Congress and tell the truth. They are certainly aware of the treatment Gen. John Singlaub received. I think the situation must be very bad indeed for young officers to be willing to risk their careers in an attempt to change it.

A second problem the volunteer army concept has created is a generally lower quality of personnel in terms of educational ability. As we all know, high school diplomas are no longer a reliable indication of knowledge and ability. Your military services are having to rewrite training manuals to an almost elementary school level and divert personnel to set up remedial reading programs for recruits.

The military medical services have suffered grievously without a draft. The rewards of private practice are simply too great to attract enough doctors into the military service. Again, Congressman Beard's study detailed the loss of morale which poor military medical service is creating.

The all-volunteer concept also puts us dangerously close to the concept of a mercenary army. History has shown time and again that the mercenary, the man who fights for money, is simply not a reliable soldier.

It's true that the Marine Corps and the Air Force have generally always relied on volunteers but our appeal was never on the basis of financial rewards. A man who volunteers to serve his country is the best kind of soldier; a man who volunteers to get a job is not.

A further defect in the all-volunteer concept has been the disastrous effect it has had on the Army Reserve and National Guard. They are dangerously under-strength and suffer even more from shortages of equipment and lack of training.

The present plans—dictated by the all-volunteer concept and budget limitations—call for immediate mobilization and deployment of the Guard and Reserve units in the event of war. The kind of war that will be fought in Europe will result in extremely high casualty rates in a relatively short period of time. There simply will not be time to re-start the draft and feed men into the training cycle.

I will not mince any words. When you take an American boy and put him on the battlefield, out of condition, poorly trained, with inadequate equipment and weapons, you are committing first degree murder. Today, many of our regular active duty men are inadequately trained and poorly equipped. What do you think will happen to a young man who is called away from his civilian job one day and finds himself on a battlefield ten days later? It will be a slaughter.

This sorry state of our conventional forces is perhaps a greater danger than our strategic weakness. Strategic forces are trump cards and they will not be lightly played for small stakes. It is the weakness of our conventional forces which will tempt the Soviets to embark on dangerous adventures which will both increase the likelihood of nuclear war or, in the absence of nuclear war, achieve for the Soviets the same goal—our surrender. Using conventional forces alone, the Soviets could force us into an untenable situation in which our only alternatives are a suicidal nuclear response or surrender.

There is no excuse for our political leaders having placed us in this vulnerable position. As a nation we have the wealth, the manpower, and the resources to provide the military strength we need to maintain our freedom and independence. What we have lacked is the will.

Our political leaders have chosen the way of expediency. They have wrapped themselves in a dream world of detente and strategic arms limitation treaties. They have indulged themselves in a fit of profligate spending, not on defense, but on the more politically popular domestic programs. Of our half a trillion dollar federal budget, barely one-fourth is devoted to defense.

Unfortunately, we are nearing the end of our rope. The Soviet arms build-up is continuing at a wartime pace. Soviet Leader Leonid Brezhnev has told East European Communist leaders that by 1985, the Soviet military and economic position will be overwhelming. Many of us believe that the Soviets are well ahead of their own timetable.

In fact, they have us outclassed both conventionally and strategically at this moment. Their current weaknesses are the East European captive people and those nationalists within the Soviet Union itself—Ukrainians, Lithuanians, Latvians and other conquered peoples who are showing more and more open defiance. It is this internal weakness which is staying the Kremlin's hand and forcing it to seek a situation where it can bluff us into surrender without actually committing its forces to combat.

That is a guess, of course, based on contacts with the dissident movement. The Soviet Union is currently taking steps to crush these brave rebels, and so prudence tells us that we must not waste a minute of the time they are buying for us with their courage.

I believe the American people are willing to pay the price for real peace and freedom. Several national polls have indicated that they are. What the American people need to know is the true situation and that is the purpose of this book.

We must get busy and elect a congress that will have the courage to tell us the truth: that we cannot have both guns and butter and that unless we cut spending on the butter and spend more on guns, we will not survive as a free and independent nation.

We must re-institute a draft, though not the same unfair system we had before. A draft should be absolutely fair so that every American male, upon reaching 18 or high school graduation, can serve two years in the cause of defending his country. There should be no exemptions except for extreme family hardship. Those not physically able to serve two years in a military service should spend two years in some type of civilian public service job. We cannot allow a system which spares the wealthy and the politically well-connected from the sacrifices necessary to achieve our common goal.

To re-arm and to re-institute the draft will take time. I doubt if either is possible with the present congress. In the meantime, there is something we can do and that is provide the American infantryman with a decent rifle and superior training and bring those dependents home.

The M-16, 5.6 mm .22 caliber rifle which is now standard in the American armed forces is not an adequate weapon. Beyond 350 meters it is almost totally ineffective. The Russian AK-47, .30 caliber, is accurate to 550 meters. The M-16 is too light to be used with the bayonet or as a club in hand-to-hand fighting. It is worthless against even light armor.

I have talked with many infantrymen and they have no confidence in this weapon. We have already on hand over 700,000 M-14, .30 caliber rifles and we must get these into the hands of our troops, especially those in Europe, and train them to use them.

The .30 caliber round, loaded with the new armor-piercing slugs, can penetrate all of the Russian equipment except their tanks. If we give our boys protective clothing and gas masks, the very best training, and a .30 caliber rifle with armor-piercing ammunition, they can stop that Soviet armored division (there are several points on a Soviet tank that are vulnerable to the .30 caliber armor-piercing bullets).

This one move, using equipment already available, will make a striking difference in the combat readiness and the morale of our European-based soldiers. Those who have been on the battlefield know that there is no substitute for a highly-trained, highly-motivated and well-equipped foot soldier. A soldier who is well-trained and has confidence in his weapon and in his buddy can overcome all sorts of technological disadvantages.

We cannot escape the hostility and aggressive intentions of the Soviet Union. Blind faith in disarmament treaties and detente is childish nonsense, equivalent to the blind faith otherwise intelligent leaders of France placed in the Maginot Line.

We must arm ourselves and arm in a hurry. We have put our sons and daughters in harm's way and to fail to give them the absolute best in weapons and leadership is to commit murder. I want the American people to understand that the individual members of the Congress, the Senate, the White House, and Defense Department are directly responsible for that murder if it occurs. It is one thing to ask a boy to give his life for his country; it is another to throw his life away because a politician lacks the guts to tell his constituents the truth and to vote for the weapons and training he needs in order to have any hope of survival.

I wish I could say that the political irresponsibility ends with the defense situation. Unfortunately, the same lack of guts, the same wishful thinking, the same love of expediency, has almost destroyed our domestic economy. We will take a look at the damage done to it in the next chapter.

Chapter III

Our Deepening Dependence

America's productive capacity and economic strength was the miracle of World War II. From July, 1940, to July 1945, American factories and shipyards produced 5,425 merchant ships; 296,601 military aircraft; 71,060 naval ships; 86,388 tanks; and 2.7 million machine guns. Truly, we were the arsenal of democracy.

Many Americans believe that nothing has changed, that we still have that great productive capacity. We don't. Our economic base has been eroding concurrently with our military power. Once more, it's time to look the truth in the eye and ponder the situation our politicians are too fearful to face.

Our currency is rapidly eroding in value; our economy is beset with high unemployment and inflation; for the first time in this century our balance of trade (how much we export and how much we import) shows a deficit; much of our productive capacity has closed down or is antiquated; and we have become dependent, not only on the import of oil, but also on the import of a number of strategic minerals and metals.

Let's examine these problem areas one by one and see just where we stand. Inflation is obvious to everyone. It really began to take off in 1973, though we've been inflating at a slower rate since World War II. Between 1973 and 1977, however, the consumer price index rose 41 per cent. Food soared 53 per cent; energy jumped 70 per cent; the cost of medical care increased 44 per cent; and the price of owning a new home rose nearly 50 per cent.

The best way to understand inflation is to realize that money—a dollar bill, for example—is not really wealth. Wealth consists of things like clothing, food, energy, and housing. Money is a medium of exchange. How much real wealth you can exchange for a dollar is what economists call purchasing power. We are accustomed to thinking of inflation in terms of price increases. Another way to think of it is in terms of a decrease in the purchasing power of a dollar. In other words, rising prices mean that each dollar is less valuable.

The question is, why does this occur? The government is expanding the money supply faster than this country is producing real wealth. All these extra dollars are used to bid up the prices of goods and services. In the German Weimar Republic in the 1920s, the government printed so many marks that they became worthless. It took a wheelbarrow full of them to buy a loaf of bread.

Our government, which controls the amount of money in circulation, has increased that amount far in excess of the available goods and services through deficit spending and by direct increases in the money supply by the Federal Reserve System. This has been the primary cause of inflation.

As of this writing, there is no sign that the government intends to stop it, though there is always a lot of deceptive rhetoric coming out of Washington. Inflation, which is a result of politicians who wish to spend more than they have the nerve to pay for by levying taxes, squeezes every American, young and old.

One study has shown that while the take-home pay of a worker with three dependents has increased from $90.86 in 1967 to $172.93 in 1977, the worker's $172.93 will buy only as much as $95.12 did in 1967. In other words, inflation has consumed all but $4.26 of the sum total of all his raises over the last ten years. To work ten years for a $4.26 a week increase is terrible. It's no wonder

America's workers are unhappy and disillusioned.

Now let's look at our trade deficit. In 1977, it was estimated at nearly $30 billion and was a historic high. That meant we imported goods worth $30 billion more than the value of the goods we exported. This contributes to the decline of the value of the dollar as foreigners end up with huge accumulations of U.S. dollars. This means we end up paying more for imports.

Oil accounts for part of the problem. Our oil imports are now about 47 per cent of our total daily consumption. In 1968 we spent $2.5 billion on oil imports; by 1976, the bill was $32 billion—thanks not only to increased volume but to larcenous price increases by the oil cartel known as OPEC.

But during that same period of time, automobile imports increased 400 per cent and imports of other consumer goods increased from a total of $5.5 billion in 1968 to $18.5 billion in 1976.

When free international trade is working well, it benefits all the nations engaged in it, and creates more jobs overall than are lost to foreign competition. However, when imports and exports become severely imbalanced because of inflation or other government-created factors, the economy suffers. Our inflation is steadily eroding our overseas markets.

Here again our problem is largely self-inflicted. American banks and corporations have direct foreign investments of nearly $26 billion. Our own political leaders have encouraged this outflow of American capital by, in many cases, guaranteeing foreign loans and insuring American investments against confiscation by foreign governments.

The fact remains that when a large American corporation shuts down an American plant and moves it to Mexico, Mexicans go to work and Americans go on the unemployment rolls.

The absurdity of our government's position is no better illustrated than in the case of oil. An American corporation can get U.S. government guarantees for loans to explore for oil in a foreign country, but if it wishes to explore in the U.S., all it gets from the government is harassment from the Environmental Protection Agency and the dozens of other regulatory agencies.

It is estimated, in fact, that government regulations add 30 to 40 per cent to the cost of everything Americans purchase and every service they engage. That is on top of the monetary inflation, also government caused, and the taxes which also make up a hefty portion of the price of everything we buy. It has been a major factor in pricing us out of many foreign markets.

Now let's look at the situation with minerals and metals. Eight mineral cartels now exist which influence to some extent the prices of petroleum, copper, tin, bauxite, lead, mercury, tungsten, and iron. As I pointed out earlier, we are dependent, in many instances, on imports. For example, we import about 47 per cent of our petroleum; 17 per cent of our copper; 86 per cent of our tin; 91 per cent of bauxite (aluminum); 14 per cent of lead; 46 per cent of mercury; 28 per cent of our tungsten; 33 per cent of iron ore; 100 per cent of our strontium; 98 per cent of manganese; 97 per cent of our cobalt; and 89 per cent of our chromium.

To sum up, we import more than 75 per cent of our twelve most needed minerals; more than 50 per cent of our eighteen most needed minerals; and 33 per cent of our twenty-seven most needed.

By far, the majority of these minerals as well as the oil, comes to our shores by ship. As we saw in the preceding chapter, we have forced our Navy to a dangerously low level of capability. Could we insure the continued import of these supplies in time of war? I think the answer is fairly obvious. No, not with the limited number of ships, aircraft and personnel we have now in our Navy. The Soviet Union has today according to Admiral Isaac Kidd, the Former Supreme Allied Commander of Naval Forces, Atlantic, the capability to disrupt our sea lanes. We have thrown away our ability to stop them.

How did all this happen? Why did we allow our nation to become so vulnerable? I believe the answer lies in part with our leadership, or rather lack of it. In the early 1950s, President Truman commissioned a blue ribbon panel of experts to look at our mineral needs. It did an outstanding job. The report was published, predicting our present problems, but no action was ever taken.

In the meantime, we drifted politically further and further away from the concepts of free enterprise and limited government. We elected congressmen and senators who did not share those beliefs. People who did not believe in free enterprise and limited government flowed into the bureaucracy—into the departments, into the staffs, into the universities, and from there into the teaching professions and into the press.

Without ever realizing what we were doing, without ever putting the question squarely to a vote of the American people, we drifted into collectivism. Ideas that would have once provoked a storm of protest gradually came to be accepted. Ideas such as empowering the government to tell private businesses what they can charge for their products and how much they have to pay their employees. Ideas such as a government five-year economic plan.

From the valid concept of limited regulation in the public interest, which was merely an extension of the traditional idea of government as a policeman, we drifted into regulation for the sake of regulation and a federal government devoted to manipulating the economy and business for political and ideological purposes.

The Carter administration's response to the energy crisis is a good example. The traditional American approach would have been to permit private enterprise, in quest of profits, to develop new energy sources freely, without interference.

Instead, the government went to academic circles and approached the entire problem with a hostile attitude toward our own businessmen. When Arabs raised the price of their oil, politicians stood up in the United States Senate and proposed that the government punish American oil producers by imposing price controls on their oil!

The same government which imposes a price for domestic natural gas so low that it discourages new production, entered into negotiations with foreign nations and proposed to pay them a much higher price.

The same government which is seeking to impose heavy taxes on domestic American oil and is urging us to conserve fuel is hampering the development of oil refineries and nuclear power plants with excessive environmental regulations. Furthermore, it is making it more and more difficult for industry to extract minerals from existing mines and is at the same time, moving to place millions and millions of acres of public land out of the reach of any exploration and development at all.

Thus, it seems no exaggeration to say that our government is pushing us toward greater and greater dependence on foreign imports at the very time our national survival is threatened by a hostile nation with the military capability to isolate us from the source of these imports.

I cannot believe such a potentially suicidal course is deliberate on the part of everyone in our government. Rather, I think it is the result of our carelessness in electing leaders who in turn appoint irresponsible, incapable, and unreliable persons to key positions. We have people regulating mines who have no practical knowledge of mining and who are hostile toward the people who do—the people in the mining industry. The same is true in oil, in forest products, in defense material procurement.

The greatest resource our nation has—the men and women in private industry who have an abundance of practical knowledge, ingenuity and energy, have all but been thrown out of Washington. Their counsel is not sought. Occasionally, they are summoned to appear and defend themselves from the attacks of shameless demagogues.

No, the great industrial miracle of World War II could not be repeated—even if we were given the time, which in the nuclear age, we will not be allowed. American industry has been strangled by government regulation and taxation, harassed at home and encouraged to go abroad.

In World War II, our industry could produce 86,000 tanks in four years. Today, the lead time for developing a new tank and producing 3,000 is close to twelve years. The change has occurred because of government bureaucracy. Franklin Roosevelt led us through World War II with a staff of about forty people. The peacetime staff of the president today is in excess of 1,500.

It is this enormous growth of government, merely typified by a swollen White House staff, which is smothering private initiative and our industrial capacity. Taxes now consume nearly 45 cents of every dollar earned. One year's interest on the national debt today is equivalent to the entire federal budget in 1941. One

American corporation has estimated it must send in, on an annual basis, 24,000 pages of reports to forty-two different government agencies. Think of the wasted manpower!

The future is not entirely black, however. The people of California staged the modern equivalent of the Boston Tea Party when they voted overwhelmingly for Proposition 13 which slashed their property taxes 60 per cent!

This is the answer. The government must be brought under control by the American people and the only way to do that is to impose limits on its spending power. There is a bill before congress that would cut federal income taxes 30 per cent and there are other resolutions, born out of the Proposition 13 excitement, to limit government spending.

Government has grown fat and inefficient. We need to return to a government that will efficiently and effectively encourage, not inhibit, our national economic growth.

This great nation and our prosperity were created by private businesses and individuals, not by government. Government exists by taking wealth created by others. It itself does not create wealth and cannot except for the false wealth of the printing press dollar bill.

We have the talent and the ingenuity to solve our energy problems, to develop the mineral and metal resources we need, and to restore our industrial capacity. Free enterprise is a giant. What we, the people, must do, is free this friendly giant from the chains of government, for never before have we so desperately needed its help.

Chapter IV

The Collapse of Courage

We have taken a hard look at three areas of national weakness: strategic forces, conventional forces, and the economy. It is time to look at one more area of weakness.

In my military experience, I have learned that unit strength depends upon individual strength. There is no such thing as a strong unit made up of weak individuals. Unity of action provides impact, but the unit's strength can never exceed the sum of the individual members' strengths. As we learned in geometry, the whole is equal to the sum of the parts.

If someone were to ask me to explain what the American nation is, I would reply immediately: 216 million individual American citizens. If someone asked me what was going to determine the future of America, I would reply immediately: the sum effect of their 216 million individual decisions.

Sadly, many of our fellow Americans have lost their sense of direction. We see the effects of their individual decisions and actions in the high crime rate, in the number of illegitimate births, in the venereal disease rate, in the disintegration of the family, in the bill for welfare services, in the books, movies, and television shows they support, and in the political corruption and malfeasance.

27

I headed a study for a senate committee on the worldwide narcotics trade. Tons of narcotics flow into the United States every year, much of it produced by our enemies, the Chinese Communists, for the double purpose of earning revenue for China and weakening this nation. An individual who becomes a drug abuser—and it doesn't matter which drug—is of no value to the nation. Worse, the individual is a liability. Someone else has to take care of him and assume his share of the total responsibility.

Drug abuse naturally is an escape mechanism, an attempt to alter reality to something more bearable or desirable than what exists. It is ironic that the nation which has made a reality of what so many still only dream of—political freedom and economic opportunity—has so many individuals who wish to escape from it.

Our judgment of reality, our decision whether it's good or bad, depends more on our value system inside our own heads than on the objective reality. Let me give you an example. A cold potato is a cold potato. The potato itself cannot change. Its taste and its consistency and its temperature remain the same. Yet, to a hungry man, that potato can taste delicious and to a man with a full stomach, it can taste so repulsive that he gags on it. The same reality—different judgments based on different values.

A value is anything we desire to acquire and to keep. It can be tangible or intangible. As we mature as individuals, we accumulate a set of values, a collection of things we desire to acquire and to keep. It is our values which determine our actions. If we adopt money as a value, then we set out to acquire and to keep it. If we desire the love of another human being, then we set out to acquire it and to retain it.

Because values become our personal objectives, it is possible to acquire both more values than we can achieve and values which are contradictory. Either condition results in frustration. If we place a high value on leisure and a high value on money and we don't happen to have been born rich, we have a conflict in values. It's very difficult to acquire money and to enjoy a lot of leisure at the same time.

We may value money, fame, health, and great accomplishments in some sport, but because of the circumstances of our birth and our physical limitations, be unable to achieve them. Here again, frustration is the result.

If you think about this, you will realize that the key to a happy life lies more inside our heads than in the external world. We cannot exert total control over the external world, but we can, in fact, exert substantial control over our minds. We can, and do, make the decisions as to what we will value and what we will not value.

Furthermore, these values can change. We can change our minds and reject old values and adopt new ones or merely add to our present store. We can also arrange our values in order of priority. In other words, we value some things more than others; often we make decisions based on these priorities.

It is fashionable in some segments of our society today to de-value heroism and one of the ways this is done is to assert that heroic acts are merely acts of insanity. I have seen too much heroism to accept such cynicism. Heroism is a result of just what we've been talking about, value systems.

I have seen thousands of young men go to their deaths, not because they did not value their lives, but because they valued other things more than their lives. Sometimes it was duty, often it was the life of a buddy, for most it was love of country.

What I have been leading up to is that a nation is a reflection of the values of the individuals who make up that nation. We still have freedom and independence in this nation today because a majority of our individual citizens have always in the past valued those two things enough to fight for them and die for them. We will remain free and independent only so long as this remains true.

The fourth major weakness of our nation today is that too many of our fellow citizens no longer value freedom and independence; some don't value them at all and others place them rather low in their priorities. The man who says "better red than dead" is stating his priorities. He values his life more than he values freedom and independence. Too many people in too many positions of leadership today reflect that kind of priority.

How did this situation come about? Well, we do not choose our values in a vacuum, though theoretically I suppose we could. We are constantly being offered values from other sources. We adopt some of these. Some values we adopt from our parents; others, from our teachers; some from friends; others, from our culture as reflected in movies, television, newspapers, and books.

The culture in the United States today reflects fundamentally a materialistic set of values: money, things which money can buy, physical comfort, things which satisfy our senses. Our culture is telling us that man was born to be well-fed, sensually satisfied, and pleasantly amused.

The strange thing is that we have achieved that state and yet there is widespread unhappiness. Looking at it on a worldwide scale, no other people have achieved the material comforts that we have. Starvation is not a problem in our society. By and large, neither is health. We spend billions on amusement and recreation. In our nation, even most people at the low rung on the economic ladder have cars, food, and television sets.

In fact, so great has been our success in this area that we have totally lost our perspective. Our official definition of poverty is far above the standard of living for billions of people. We have, with sanitation and medical care, greatly extended the productive years of our people; yet there seems to be constant grumbling about our private health care system.

The problem lies, I believe, in adopting the materialistic set of values. The human being is mortal. As soon as we are born, we begin an unstoppable cycle of growth and decay leading to death. In the face of this slow and inevitable decline in our physical bodies, material pleasures must inevitably turn vinegary and un-satisfying. We can buy neither eternal youth nor immortality. If cars, houses, cash, sex, and food have been our highest values, then as they lose their allure, as they do in the shadow of ap-proaching death, we are left with an emptiness and bitterness, so well expressed by the popular song, "Is That All There Is?" Indeed, we ask ourselves, is that all there is to life?

More to the point of our interest in a strong national defense, people whose values are solely materialistic are reluctant to take risks. If indeed material pleasures are all there is to life, why die any sooner than you have to; why subject yourself to any unpleasantness; why take any risks? Thus materialism breeds a certain cowardice so well summed up by the expression, "better red than dead."

Ours is not the first culture to adopt materialism; there is a history of many. And each one fell. There is no great mystery as to why. First, the materialist will always be defensive since it is always his goal to preserve and to protect his material comforts. This forfeits to the foe the strategic advantages of the offense. Secondly, the materialist will always look for the easy way, for a compromise or a trade-off or a sellout. Finally, the man who has his own physical preservation as his highest value, will lack the commitment and conviction necessary to win in a struggle with a foe who does not fear death or hardship.

We can see these symptoms of materialism throughout our society, but the most visible one is loss of courage. People stand by and watch a fellow citizen being beaten or stabbed and they do not interfere. They are afraid. Our political leaders watch communism gobble up other nations and they do nothing. They are afraid. People complain in private about the state of affairs but will not speak out in public. They are afraid.

Fear and courage are both reflections of value systems. The coward values his life more than his honor or his duty and so flees from danger. The brave man values his honor and duty more than his life and so faces danger. The brave man is no more eager to die than the coward; he simply values other things more than his life so that when faced with a choice, he chooses to risk his life rather than sacrifice his other values.

The traditional American values have been larger than materialism. For most of the history of this nation, we have been poor. The men who signed the Declaration of Independence were for the most part wealthy and prosperous. They had achieved their prosperity as loyal subjects of the British Crown. Certainly, if prosperity had been their highest value, they would have remained British subjects and fought to defend the status quo. Yet they opted for freedom and independence because these were indeed their highest values and to achieve them, they sacrificed their prosperity and in some cases, their lives.

There is another quality those early Americans shared, too, and that was belief in a Supreme Being. Over and over again in their public and private papers, you see references to God.

The trouble with materialism is that it places the individual at the center of the Universe and this is as great a mistake in thinking as that committed by those earlier men who placed the earth in the center of the universe with all the stars revolving around it.

When you cut through the rationalizations, a Universe without God has only one logical message for man: that he is an insignificant and meaningless nit who appears briefly on a small cinder lost in the vastness of space. It is no wonder that those who adopt materialism and reject the concept of Supreme Being end up miserable despite their frantic efforts to satiate their senses. Materialism is the ancient philosophy of hedonism—eat, drink, and be merry for tomorrow we die—dressed up in modern verbiage.

I do not believe that the majority of Americans accept materialism despite the universal advocacy of it by many of their political, intellectual, and artistic leaders. We are, as a people, better than the leaders we have produced. Most Americans retain the old values—belief in God, love of freedom and independence, and respect for their fellow man, but too many of us have allowed ourselves to be intimidated by the culture-makers and have not asserted our values.

The revolution that is necessary to turn this nation away from weakness toward strength must occur in the heart and mind of each citizen. We must think clearly and establish our values and our priorities and we must assert them. We must have the courage of our convictions, the courage to tell the world, "This is what I believe and I will not be bullied, frightened, intimidated or overcome. Nor will I tolerate leaders who espouse the opposite of my beliefs."

If we will do this, not only will we see our nation overcome its weaknesses and trials, but we, as individuals, will find that indeed there is a great deal more to life; that the pleasure of having made ourselves a better human being than the one who started life's journey will sustain us and strengthen us to the end—which is only the beginning of the beyond.

Chapter V

Who Calls the Shots?

When I landed in Korea, first as commander of the 5th Marine Regiment, I was certainly unaware that we were destined for a bloody war of attrition rather than fighting to win, though events convinced me that this was indeed the unspoken policy.

At the time, I was politically naive. Like all American military professionals, it had been drummed into my head that politics was the province of civilians. My job was to fight—someone else would decide who and when and under what conditions. Little did I dream that the civilian leadership was willing to sacrifice American lives in no-win wars and to keep this policy secret from the American people.

It happened in Korea. It happened in Vietnam.

As you know, American forces in Korea were under United Nations command. (They still are.) It first began to dawn on me that something was drastically wrong as a result of my own combat experiences. I was a colonel then and not privy to the frustrations that were besetting our high command.

I think most of us were shocked and angry when General Douglas MacArthur was relieved of his command. We in the Marines were even more shocked and angry when our 1st Marine Division had completed its drive to the Yalu River and then were faced

with hordes of Chinese Communist Army forces who were form-
ing and attacking from a U.N.-imposed sanctuary north of the
Yalu. Both before and after they crossed, we were denied the use
of our artillery and air power to prevent their massing for attack
into Korea. Our forces were ordered to withdraw to the U.N.-
imposed Demarcation Military Zone line.

Once we manned that line to defend South Korea from further
incursions by the North Koreans and Chinese, we had further
restrictions placed on our forces. I was a regimental commander
on that line from late October, 1952, until the summer of 1953.
We were dug-in in trenches and bunkers on a lineal defense line
nose to nose with Communist Chinese Forces one-half to three-
quarters of a mile away.

Artillery, mortar and machine gun fire from the Communists
was a constant and deadly harassment. We returned the fire in
kind—but were limited in the number of artillery and mortar shells
we could fire no matter how intense the enemy action was!

The Chinese also made heavy infantry attacks against our positions and although we were always able to repel these attacks,
it was not without considerable casualties on both sides. In an
effort to destroy the enemy's ability to make these attacks, we
planned numerous offensive attacks against their heavily de-
fended, entrenched and bunkered positions. Time and again we
captured their strongholds and could have held them, but each
time we were ordered by U.N. Headquarters Command to relinquish control and fall back to our own lines.

It bothered me deeply that I was required to submit twenty-four
hours in advance a detailed plan of attack for approval by U.N.
Command Headquarters. It bothered me because it soon became
apparent that each time we attacked, the enemy was waiting for
us. Only by a supreme effort and teamwork on the part of my
Marines were we able to win our objective and defeat the local
enemy forces. We were literally in a *Catch 22* situation. We could
not achieve surprise. We could not retain anything we won. But
we could not afford not to attack, for if we had not, the Chinese
would have been able to build up their forces to overwhelming
numbers which could have then broken through our lines and

annihilated our forces. We had to keep them off balance. The Chinese fought under no U.N. restrictions.

One evening in early March, one of my radiomen intercepted a Communist Chinese message which indicated they were planning a heavy attack against the center of my regimental position shortly after midnight. This time, I did not report this to higher headquarters—for two reasons: first, we had only an indication and weren't sure, but secondly, if it was good information, I intended to take full advantage of it.

At 12:30 A.M., I requested flares from a plane circling overhead. I was in my front line observation post, a radio transmitter in my hand connecting me to nine batteries of artillery and one battery of five-inch rockets. The eerie light of the flares revealed a mass of humanity, over a thousand Chinese soldiers, moving toward our lines and only 600 to 800 yards away. They started a charge and I gave the order to fire. Every Marine on the line opened up and all ten batteries fired simultaneously. It was the end of the world, literally, for those Chinese. They never reached our line.

A lucky radio intercept had saved the lives of many Americans. The next morning, however, a reprimand sizzled down from U.N. Command Headquarters. I had failed to notify them of the intercept and I had fired too many artillery rounds!

We could, of course, have won the Korean War, but victory was not the goal of the U.N. officials who manipulated events. I didn't realize it at the time, but the United Nations structure makes sure that the under-secretary of the Security Council who is responsible for military matters is always from the Soviet bloc.

General MacArthur, in his book, *Reminisences*, goes into detail about the frustrations he had to deal with. In describing his meeting with President Harry Truman on Wake Island, MacArthur notes that Truman, who had begun the war so decisively and aggressively, seemed unsure of himself: "The original courageous decision of Harry Truman to boldly meet and defeat communism in Asia was apparently being chipped away by the constant pounding whispers of timidity and cynicism."

Twenty years later I would hear from the mouth of another President, Lyndon Johnson, bitter words about the advice he had received from some of his civilian aides that resulted in another no-win situation in Vietnam.

I cannot help but feel deeply and bitterly about the tremendous sacrifices made by hundreds of thousands of young Americans—for what? To fight a war of attrition, a stalemate? This is the most immoral kind of war, resulting in enormous casualties, civilian and military, and needless destruction to the country being fought in. There is indeed no substitute for victory nor can a nation such as ours, which depends on the citizen soldier, commit its sons to a no-win war without inflicting unbearable and lasting damage on their morale and the overall effectiveness of its military forces. Our sons are patriots, not mercenaries, and patriots cannot be asked to kill for the sake of killing or die for no good reason without very serious repercussions.

War is my profession. I know its hellish nature. No man should be made to endure its horrors except to accomplish a goal which is equivalent in value to life itself. It is an American military tradition that each single American life is precious and must not under any circumstances be squandered. Stalemate and appeasement are contrary to our traditions and are not goals men will willingly fight or die for.

Political decisions, however, had already set in motion events for which we would pay dearly later. At Yalta and at Potsdam, Soviet dictator Joseph Stalin "won" the conferences. Russian troops occupied eastern Europe and set up puppet regimes; Germany had been divided, and no access to Berlin had been provided for in the agreements. Just six days before the atomic bomb was dropped and fourteen days before Japan agreed to surrender, President Truman asked the Russians to declare war on Japan. They did and moved their troops into Manchuria, North Korea, and the northern Japanese islands.

Some were aware of the problems the Communists would cause, but in the hubbub of victory, those warnings were ignored. Winston Churchill, Britain's great wartime leader, sent his famous "iron curtain" message in May, 1945, warning Truman of the dangers. By July, though, the British had turned Winnie out, opting instead for a socialist government.

By 1948, Communist regimes were entrenched in all of Eastern Europe. The Russians were challenging us, with the Berlin Blockade, to abandon that city, and at the same time precipitating a civil war in Greece. A year later, China fell to the Communists and the year after that, North Korea invaded South Korea and Americans were once more on a battlefield, slogging in the mud and fighting the dirty war the infantry must always fight.

We had, of course, demobilized as is our tradition and so by 1950 were hardly more prepared to fight a war than we had been in 1941. I cannot entirely blame our leaders for that situation, however. That is part of the American tradition of the citizen-soldier. I have led these "short-timers" in three wars and there is no better or more dedicated fighting man in the world. Still, when the last shot is fired, he is eager to go home. Ours is not a militaristic nation nor would I wish it to be.

I do blame the leadership for not insisting that those who did remain in uniform be trained. Hard training and tough discipline are a way of life in the Marine Corps and I have seen the results in lives saved on the battlefield. I feel that it is an act of gross neglect and unadulterated murder on the part of a government, a military service, or an officer to knowingly and willfully commit unconditioned, untrained, or ill-equipped men to the field of battle.

Despite the Korean War there is a tendency today to look back upon the 1950s as an era of stability and safety. Actually, the wrong thinking that had been done in the late 1940s had already begun to undermine our security. It simply wasn't as visible in the 1950s as it is today.

The advent of nuclear weapons genuinely frightened many influential Americans to the point that they feared, as strange as it seems, an American nuclear monopoly. It was actually proposed by some Americans that the United States turn over to the United Nations all of its atomic technology and that the U.N. build in several countries, including the USSR, nuclear facilities.

Our weapons were to be destroyed and any new nuclear weapons would be outlawed by the international agency. The Soviet Union, because it had already stolen or otherwise acquired much of the technology and was in the process of building its own atomic weapons, rejected the scheme. Here is another instance where many young Americans today, because they are not being taught history, are misled into believing that their country initiated the confrontation with communism that for a time was called the Cold War. Instead of using our nuclear monopoly, we offered to give it up!

Many clear thinkers at that time realized that there was no way to peacefully co-exist with the Soviet Union and that it was bent on world conquest. Unfortunately, they were not listened to. Instead, a policy was decided upon that deliberately gave up our one military advantage and committed us to no-win wars, the latest of which was Vietnam.

This was documented by the release of National Security Council Memorandum No. 68, when it was declassified after twenty-five years. In essence, it set the course of our foreign policy history up until the present. While recognizing the aggressive aims of the Soviet Union, NSC 68 committed us to avoiding a nuclear war, even to the extent of accepting a Soviet first strike. Secondly, it committed us to confining our military actions to limited counteractions. Thirdly, it advocated seeking co-existence in the hope that the Soviet Union would gradually evolve into a more compatible world partner. Fourth, it committed us to a policy of "containment" but of never "directly challenging Soviet prestige."

This document was based on the analysis and policies advocated by George F. Kennan, first drafted by him in 1945 while he was charge d'affaires at the U.S. embassy in Moscow with Ambassador Averell Harriman. While it was later replaced by other written policies, the basic philosophy of NSC 68 continues to dominate our government to this day.

The American public, and indeed the vast majority of the American military officers, were never aware that we had decided unilaterally to forfeit the initiative in the war with communism, in effect, to give up our technological superiority, and doom our men to fight in no-win wars at the time and place of the Communists' choice.

To put it in plain language, there have existed at least since 1945, two American policies—one public and one unspoken. The public policy has expressed the traditional ideals we all believe in—the right of people to be free, self-defense, peace through strength, opposition to communism. The unspoken policy has expressed the thinking of the advisers who have influenced every American president—selling out oppressed peoples, unilateral moves towards disarmament, and accommodation with communism.

Publicly, we were committed to defend ourselves and others against Communist aggression. Privately, we intended to appease it. We let Eastern Europe and China fall into Communist hands at a time we possessed the power to save them both. We publicly preached liberation of the Captive Nations but when the East Germans, the Poles, the Hungarians, the Czechs revolted, we did nothing while the Soviet Union crushed them.

Publicly we were committed to preserving freedom in Indochina and as in Korea, we even went through the motions of fighting for it, tragically expending over 50,000 American lives—but, as in Korea, we were denied the opportunity to win the war. Cambodia, Laos, and South Vietnam are now Communist slave camps.

Publicly we were committed to the Monroe Doctrine, but we did not prevent Cuba from being turned into a Soviet military base and we have now given away the Panama Canal.

In the 1960s and 1970s these unspoken policies took a new turn. Robert McNamara, former secretary of defense and now president of the World Bank, began the process of gradual unilateral disarmament though he never admitted publicly that that was what we were doing.

We moved from a strategy of deterrence involving the capacity to win a nuclear war, even after absorbing a first strike, to the concept of Mutual Assured Destruction which involves minimum deterrence and exposing American cities to attack.

As in all cases, actions follow ideas. The origin of the new idea that deterrence should be decoupled from the capacity to win a nuclear war was spelled out recently by Maj. Gen. Dale O. Smith, USAF (ret.) in the *Journal of International Relations*.

In 1960, according to General Smith, the American Academy of Arts and Sciences and the Twentieth Century Fund sponsored a Summer Study on Arms Control at Harvard and Massachusetts Institute of Technology.

The concept which emerged from this study was that an arms race would lead to less security. From that, corollary ideas followed: arms control was more important than war-winning ability, there is a greater risk in the arms race than in disarmament, the arms race would inevitably lead to war, nuclear parity was safer than nuclear superiority.

Actions followed ideas. In 1961, the congress established the U.S. Arms Control and Disarmament Agency. With key civilians in the Defense Department, the State Department, the White House staff and the congress supporting this basket of concepts, the slow disarmament of the United States began.

Roswell Gilpatrick, McNamara's deputy, spelled it out in an article in *Foreign Affairs*, the journal of the Council on Foreign Relations, which was published in 1964 after his retirement. Gilpatrick called for all manned bombers to be retired from active deployment, the phaseout of all manned interceptors and all other bomber defenses and no production of an anti-ballistic missile system.

With the exception of the remaining B-52s and FB-111s, Gilpatrick's ideas have now become fact. Dr. Jerome B. Wiesner, former science adviser; McGeorge Bundy, former special assistant for national security affairs; William C. Foster, former deputy secretary of defense; Harold Brown, our present secretary of defense, were leaders of the disarmament movement.

The propaganda umbrella under which most of this was done was detente. Let's examine this concept in detail. It is a French word that means simply easing strained relations. As a policy, it involved negotiating arms agreements with the Soviets, which has now put us at a disadvantage; increasing trade and credit to the Soviet Union, which helped them build their war machine; signing the Helsinki Agreement which legitimizes Soviet control of Eastern Europe; and refusing to acknowledge publicly Soviet actions which are detrimental to peace and freedom, which puts us in the ridiculous position of lamenting problems without naming the cause of the problem.

Obviously if two football teams adopted a policy of genuine detente, there would be no game. If only one of the teams adopted a policy of detente, the other team would roll over them. That is exactly our position in regard to detente with the Soviet Union. We adopted a passive, conciliatory attitude and they charged ahead with all the speed, determination and aggressiveness of an American professional football team.

No American who thinks through the situation should be surprised to find his country in a position of weakness. Suppose you owned a professional football team. What factors would determine its success? One obviously is the caliber of the players. If you hire players who are timid and inexperienced and physically weak, then the opposition teams will run over them. Another factor is strategy or thinking ability. If your coach can't think clearly, is given to daydreaming, and refuses to face facts, then disaster is guaranteed.

A nation is similar to a football team. Whether it will be a winner or a loser depends on the qualities of the individuals who make up the government. The appointed officials and advisers are the players. The president and the congress are the coaching staff.

Let's take a hard look at some of the members of our team. Perhaps then we can determine how it is we have ended up behind, on our own goal line, in the last quarter of the game, with the clock running out.

Chapter VI

The Elite in Power

As we look at some of the officials who guided our nation to its present situation of peril, I want to remind you that I promised to stick to facts and that is what I am going to do. What we are interested in is correcting our problems, not in assessing blame.

Our only point in looking back is to understand the influences which have brought us to the present, to identify the people whose faulty thinking has been so harmful to our national interests. It is not important at this point to speculate about motives.

Actually, the ideas, more than the individuals who conceive them, are most important. Ideas once accepted can continue to dominate a nation for decades—long after the people who originated them have left power.

Everything we do is a product of our thinking. To put it on the simple level of an individual, we as human beings use our brains as our principal means of survival. To survive, we must accurately identify reality and conceive of the proper course of actions necessary to adapt to reality or mold it to our designs.

It's easier to see this process in the field of science. For centuries man has been plagued with malaria. No progress was achieved in preventing it until reality—the fact that it was transmitted by a mosquito—had been correctly identified. Once that had been done, then the human mind could conceive of actions that could be taken—like draining swamps and spraying to eliminate the mosquitoes.

Domestic and foreign policies are the result of the same mental process. So are military strategy and tactics. First, you must correctly identify reality—the nature of your enemy and his forces; then you must plan actions which will cope with the battle situation that actually exists, and solve the problem.

The catch is that while the human mind is the most remarkable creation in nature, it is not error-proof. The best of minds makes mistakes. Sometimes there is not enough information available to correctly identify reality; sometimes information which is available is misinterpreted; sometimes, even when the reality is correctly identified, the actions which are taken are bungled.

Each of us can see this process with all its good and bad points at work in our own lives. We have all made mistakes. We have all at some point believed something was so only to discover later, it was not true. We have decided to do things and later found that we made the wrong decisions. We can call this the human factor, for there is no human being whose thinking is error-proof 100 per cent of the time.

Now let's move a second step. Government is made up of human beings. The fact that a man or woman is elevated to a position of great responsibility, prestige, and authority does not remove the human factor, the inability to be correct all of the time.

This is as true of generals as it is of presidents, congressmen, business executives, or scholars—even though the generals, presidents, congressmen, business executives, and scholars won't admit it.

Now let's go a step further and look more closely at government in terms of how decisions are made. First, there is the bureaucracy—the career employees. Every one of these in whatever position is a human being with his or her own unique set of attitudes, prejudices, and beliefs.

Next there are the elected officials—the congressmen, and the president on the federal level whom we charge with the responsibility for making decisions in the domestic and foreign policy fields. These, too, are human beings affected not only by the human factor but also by their own set of prejudices and attitudes which have developed as a result of their past experiences.

Congressmen and presidents, of course, do not make decisions in a vacuum. They are subject to the pressures of the office and to other influences. We, just the ordinary voters, have some influence. Their staffs and advisers have even more. The media exerts some influence. So do their families, their close friends, and their financial backers.

The one startling conclusion I've come to in analysing America today is that of all the sources of influence which feed the decision-making process, the voters are the weakest. This may strike you as unlikely, but let's examine the idea. We are accustomed to thinking that the voters manipulate the politicians in the sense of choosing who is to be a successful politician and hence influencing his decisions.

I have come to the conclusion that too often the process works in the reverse. It is the voter who is manipulated. The voter can be manipulated by being presented with a limited choice of candidates, by the information which he is presented or denied.

Another factor is that some citizens in our land of equality are more equal than others in terms of influence. Quite obviously, even on the local level, the president of a large bank can exert more influence on politicians than can the employee of a service station. The service station employee and the banker have the same vote, the same rights under the Constitution, but not the same ability to influence the decision-making process.

This may strike you as undemocratic, but it is a fact that derives from human nature. If we are going to understand our nation, we must correctly identify reality and not cling to myths. It is a fact that in the United States some people, because of their wealth or their position or their friendships with people of wealth, have a great deal of influence on the political decision-making process.

Beginning in the late 1800s, a number of families amassed huge fortunes and some of the wealthiest centered their operations in New York and Boston. Because of their great wealth, they have exerted a great deal of influence on government, private institutions like universities, and on news media.

Some writers have referred to this group of wealthy people as the Eastern Establishment and I suppose that is as good a name as any so long as you keep in mind that the Establishment is a generalized term for a rather diverse group of individuals and not a monolithic, conspiratorial group of people whose thinking is identical on every subject.

It's been well-established by a number of scholars that this Establishment has generally been the dominant influence on the executive branch of our government since the days of Woodrow Wilson. Presidents have chosen their cabinet members from it, particularly the secretaries of state and treasury. Most presidential advisers have come from it. The bulk of presidential campaign contributions have come from it. And from within it, have arisen the great newspapers and television networks, book publishing firms, and magazines which exert such great influence on the minds of all of us.

This Establishment has been the source of what Sen. Daniel Moynihan refers to as "the interlocking elites" which set American foreign policy. Therefore it has been the principal, though not the sole, source of the public men who have guided our Republic for most of this century.

Unfortunately, in many instances, the wealth and influence of these players have exceeded their judgment. Their thinking, like yours or mine, is not only subject to the human error factor but it also is colored by their backgrounds, their experiences, and their interests.

Their outlook, for example, has been consistently internationalist. This is quite natural. Much of the great wealth derives from international corporations, or multinationals, as they are called today. The Rockefeller family, to cite just one example, has business interests and assets all around the globe. Whether it is wise for us to allow them to use their international interests to heavily influence the national government is an urgent question.

Another consistent trait in the thinking of the Establishment has been a generally moderate, live-and-let-live attitude toward communism and the Soviet Union. There has been a remarkably consistent record of trade and aid to the Soviet Union beginning with the Russian Revolution, but here again I think there has been no consistency on the part of some of them as to motive or long-range purpose.

The most unfair thing we can do is to judge people out of context. Today, we have the benefit of sixty years' experience with communism and the Soviet Union. Our knowledge of its reality is far superior to the knowledge available to people in the 1920s, 1930s, and 1940s.

The thesis propounded by Kennan that the Soviet Union would eventually evolve into a nation with which we could live, may have seemed quite reasonable in 1945. What is *not* reasonable is for us today to continue to base our foreign policy on it, in the face of thirty-three years of evidence that it is incorrect.

As a source of foreign policy decision-makers, the Establishment has sometimes suffered from intellectual inbreeding, from confusing private interests with national interests, from an arrogance that often comes with great wealth, and from a lack of experience in a broad sense.

I think it is very difficult for a human being who has led a genteel, safe, and comfortable life to understand a human being whose background includes extreme hardship, terror, cruelty and savage fighting. Should we have expected a scholar like Kennan to really understand a killer like Stalin?

It was fashionable, during the great psychological warfare that was conducted in this country during the Vietnam War, to picture Establishment figures as hawkish. That, however, is totally misleading. They were hawkish only to the degree that they did not wish to totally surrender to communism, but they never once advanced a national strategy to defeat the communists, in Vietnam or anywhere else.

Their response—and they must bear the burden of our foreign policy, for they have provided the key advisers to all the presidents since 1945—is always *containment*. In effect, the dominant foreign policy decision has been to stall for time in the hope that with the passing of years some permanent accommodation could be reached.

Thus we created NATO, but had no plan eventually to push the Soviet Union back from Eastern Europe or to reduce its influence there. Thus we would retaliate but not attack. Thus, we drove the North Koreans out of South Korea but did not reunite the country. Thus we fought in South Vietnam, but not effectively in North Vietnam. Thus, on a global scale, as on a smaller scale in Korea and Vietnam, we would grant the enemy sanctuary and limit our actions to responding to his initiatives at his choice of time and place.

This strategy was based entirely on the hope that passing years would dissolve the problem by changing the Soviet Union from a monster into a tame beast. It was from the beginning a fairy tale based on inaccurate perception of the reality of communism.

Similarly, the concepts of nuclear parity and mutually assured destruction were defective. In theory, the Soviets would be allowed to achieve nuclear parity with the U.S., would therefore no longer fear us, and would then become amenable to peaceful coexistence. In actuality, the Soviets have never feared us, having discovered as early as the Berlin Crisis and again in Korea that we lacked the will to go on the offensive. Always, their hostility has been based on their world conquering ideology, not on fear.

Consequently, when we voluntarily and unilaterally scrapped our chemical and biological warfare during the Nixon administration, the Soviets doubled their efforts in these fields. When we began to unilaterally disarm by not funding or delaying modern strategic weapons systems, they embarked on an unprecedented armaments program which propelled them to nuclear and conventional superiority and which continues to this moment.

The defective thinking of those who have dominated the State and Defense Departments and the White House staffs can be traced back to the beginning. At the end of World War II, major studies were conducted of strategic bombing. Our civilian strategists were so overwhelmed and shocked by the power of the atomic bomb that they made a fundamental decision that the invention of nuclear weapons had rendered war inoperable as a policy option. To them, nuclear war was unthinkable and unwinnable.

From that basic concept flowed the other erroneous concepts—containment, deterrence, parity, mutually assured destruction, and finally the zealous belief in disarmament.

The Soviet Union also conducted studies of strategic bombing and its effects at the end of World War II. They even made a study which I read in the early 1960s, on how to counter aircraft carrier task forces and they came up with the cruise missile as the solution. In the Soviet Union, however, strategy was the province of the military and furthermore virtually all of the Soviet leadership had had direct and personal experiences in war.

Not surprisingly, Soviet thinkers drew conclusions exactly the opposite of our Wall Street and Ivy League civilians. Soviet thinkers saw the nuclear weapon for exactly what it is, just a more powerful bomb; a more effective instrument of war. They came to the conclusion that nuclear war was not only thinkable but feasible and definitely winnable.

From that basic premise have ensued all of their subsequent concepts: the decision to seek a first-strike capability; the decision to seek reload and refire capability; the decision to go for the heavy payload (necessary for first strike destruction of our siloes); the decision to invest heavily in civil defense; and the decision to design and equip all conventional forces so they can fight in a battlefield contaminated with radiation, chemical, and biological agents.

Some Americans, when they review the errors in thinking that our advisers have made, begin to question their loyalty, but I do not think that that is the issue. The human being is a subjective creature and in most cases cannot separate his thinking, his emotions, and his experiences. In short, a man's experiences, his thinking and his character are inseparable.

The errors in our strategic thinking have been the result, not of treachery, but of wishful thinking. It's simply been our misfortune that the people who emerged as the key decision-makers have not been realists. They were frightened by the atomic bomb and did not comprehend the cruelty and toughness of the Soviet leaders.

We recognize in our daily lives that people have different characters and that their actions and thinking are influenced by their character. We see that some people are tough and some are timid, some are realists, some dreamers. Character often hinges, in my opinion, on the presence of courage and clear thinking, or their absence.

I do not mean to imply that battlefield experience is necessary for national leaders. It is not. Nor are all members of the Establishment "dreamers". Sen. Daniel Moynihan is an Ivy League scholar, but he is tough. Jack Kennedy was born a millionaire, but he had courage. No, character is not a product of environment entirely.

Furthermore, courage alone is no guarantee of correct thinking, but it is a powerful aid, for the brave man will not shrink from considering all the options and all the possible solutions to a problem while others recoil from those which are dangerous, or horrible—and nuclear war is both.

It's strange, in this age of super-sophistication and technology, to ponder that the fate of nations depends so strongly on something so fundamental as a leader's character, but I believe history proves this to be a fact.

In 1978, Kennan was backed into a corner by a newspaperwoman who was interviewing him. "You're saying then," she said, "better red than dead." Kennan replied, "Rather red than dead."

So our strategy has failed for lack of realism and courage as it was bound to fail. A football team forbidden by its coaches to make any offensive plays at all must inevitably lose the game. The world is and always has been an arena and victory goes to the strong and the bold. The tragedy of our time is that we turned over the decision-making process to a group of individuals who are proven losers.

Before we leave this subject, I think there is one more point which will help us understand the history of our times. That is, how did these people acquire so much influence over foreign policy? Why did such diverse men as Harry Truman, Dwight Eisenhower, John Kennedy, Lyndon Johnson, Richard Nixon, Gerald Ford and Jimmy Carter draw from the same basic pool for so many key advisers?'

For one reason, these people have made foreign affairs an area of special interest. From the Council on Foreign Relations to the Trilateral Commission to the think tanks and institutes they have created, the Eastern Establishment has without question created a cadre of people who are knowledgeable in foreign affairs.

For another, common sense tells you that men like our presidents, all men from humble backgrounds with the exception of Kennedy, all men with modest education, could not help but be impressed by these men of immense wealth, international prestige, and enormous power. It was the case of the "boy from the sticks" being courted and flattered by the sophisticated men who represent the zenith of our materialistic society.

I think it is significant the presidents, with the exception of Carter, were fundamentally tough-minded men and that our boldest actions seemed to have been the result of their overriding their advisers. MacArthur remarked about the change in Truman as his advisers whittled away at his resolve. We've learned that the tough decisions in the Nixon administration—to mine Haiphong, for example—were made despite protests. I myself heard Johnson and Eisenhower in private conversations, complain of "the New York crowd" in discussing limitations on their actions.

I think it's fair to say that the Eastern interests, for quite honorable and natural reasons, made a decision to play an influential role in U.S. foreign policy and succeeded in dominating it.

I think it's also fair to say that, while they have succeeded in dominating it, they have failed to evolve a policy which can cope with the menace of Russian imperialism. It's not that they haven't tried. But they are men who apparently cannot understand other men who would destroy the world for the sake of an idea.

Chapter VII

The Enemies Among Us

One of the greatest Americans I have ever known, and one of the bravest, had deep religious scruples against taking a human life. He was Sen. Paul Douglas of Illinois. Paul was offered a Marine Corps commission in World War II and he accepted on the condition that he go through boot camp. He was fifty-one years old at the time and it nearly killed him, but he completed the training right along side the eighteen-year-olds.

On Pelilieu, Paul was my adjutant and I finally had to issue him an order to keep him off the front lines. He would crawl on his belly under heavy fire to take bazooka rounds and other ammunition to the Marines on the line.

One morning, after the main battle was over and we were mopping up, Paul and I went out to scout for a command post area. He took one jungle trail and I another. After I'd gone a hundred yards, I heard several shots from the direction Paul had taken; then there was an explosion. I ran back down the trail to find Paul. He was standing beside a trench leading to a machine gun emplacement, his pistol in his hand. In the trench lay three dead Japanese soldiers, victims of a hand grenade and pistol shots. Paul had single-handedly knocked out a Japanese machine gun emplacement. On his face was all the anguish of his Quaker upbring-

51

ing. He was in a state of shock from his experience.

"They tried to kill me, Colonel. I had to kill them, didn't I?"

I put my hand on his shoulder. "Yes, Paul. That's what war is about. They try to kill us and we have to kill them to save our lives."

Thirty years later, a few months before his death, I visited him at his home in Maryland. Almost the first words out of his mouth were, "Lew, I really had to kill those men, didn't I?" Paul Douglas hated war, but not more than he loved his country.

I tell this story of a traumatic experience of a great American because it is important to remember, as we discuss the psychological war that is being conducted in our country, that there are diverse forces at work. Some people, for example, have deep religious convictions that cause them to advocate disarmament and pacifism. Some people, who advocate a one-world government, do so out of the sincere belief that it is the only road to peace and the preservation of our country. The purpose of the psychological war is either to achieve or to maintain political power, or to influence those who have political power.

No reasonable person can avoid the conclusion that one of the forces at work on American public opinion is composed of Communists, both domestic activists and foreign agents. It was established in the late 1940s that some Americans, who had risen to high positions in our government, were active agents of the Soviet Union engaged in both influencing our policy and in espionage. We also have examples from other nations.

Willy Brandt, the respected chancellor of West Germany, resigned because Soviet agents were found in high places in his office. More recently, the West German defense minister resigned for the same reason. Soviet agents have, in fact, been found in high government positions in France, Switzerland, Norway, and Great Britain. The British head of counter-intelligence, Kim Philby, proved to be a Soviet agent.

It is simply unreasonable to think that the Soviets could place agents in every western government except that of the United States. Yet there have been few serious attempts to investigate this situation.

Our internal security procedures have become ineffective. Thanks to an amendment by Sen. George McGovern, known Communist terrorists can now get visas to visit the United States more easily than respected public officials of some non-Communist countries. There is hardly even an attempt made to screen appointments and job applicants for subversive activities. The ability of both the FBI and the CIA to conduct counter-intelligence activities has been reduced to almost total incapacity. All of this has come at a time in our history when the Soviet Union has stepped up its subversive activities everywhere in the world.

It is estimated that on any given day there are as many as 25,000 Communist bloc nationals in the United States—diplomats, journalists, trade representatives, academics, entertainers, sports figures, and merchant seamen. A great percentage of them are members of the Soviet KGB or are working on special assignment for the KGB.

I know from my own experience in working with a U.S. Senate committee to investigate the world narcotics trade that there are at least 5,000 Communist Chinese agents in the U.S., most of them infiltrated as merchant seamen who jump ship. These agents are engaged in supplying heroin and many of them are trained subversives.

When we are dealing with the Communists, it's very easy to identify their objectives. They wish to destroy a free America and so, like a pack of wolves in pursuit of a stag, they will do anything and everything to weaken us. They will, for example, seek to destroy the discipline and fighting spirit of our military by pushing drugs at military installations and by downgrading our national spirit among the military.

After serving a year on President Gerald Ford's Clemency Board, I became convinced that the amnesty program was in part instigated to weaken our armed forces. The staff of this board which had been assembled by former Sen. Charles Goodell was headed by a man who had a large sign on the wall in the back of his plush office desk which read, "Better Red Than Dead." I learned later that his name had been carried on lists of the House Committee on Un-American Activities before it was disbanded.

Communists can also be expected to try to divide us by aggravating race relations and encouraging anti-Semitism; they will encourage labor strife; they will propagandize against our anti-Communist allies; they will encourage us to disarm; they will push us to make diplomatic concessions to the Soviet Union; they will attack anti-Communists and promote people who are either Communists or in sympathy with Communists; they will attempt to steal our technology and our military secrets; and should hostilities break out, they will be ready to perform assassinations and sabotage. The thing to remember about Communists is that no matter how much they protest to the contrary, their primary loyalty is to a foreign power.

But Communists are only one of many groups engaged in psychological warfare. Perhaps you noticed, as I listed the Communist objectives, that several of these are the same objectives as those of the more liberal forces we have discussed earlier. This is true, and without alliances with liberals and leftists, the Communists would achieve very few of their objectives.

For example, Communists have for years sought the destruction of the House Committee on Un-American Activities. Civil libertarians in congress closed it down. Communists have long sought to weaken the FBI and CIA's anti-Communist abilities; the liberal congress and the executive branch have done the job for them. Whether it's American disarmament, sanctions against Chile, South Africa, and Rhodesia, betrayal of the free Chinese on Taiwan, or normal relations with Fidel Castro, there is too often an alignment between the goals of Communists and those of the liberal element.

Why is this? Well, one answer is that many liberals are socialists. Both Communists and socialists subscribe to a public-ownership economic philosophy; Communists merely added the revolutionary tactics of Lenin. Socialists and Communists find themselves with broad areas of agreement on objectives, differing principally on the tactics to achieve them. Socialism has become, for many socialists, a sort of religion which compels a loyalty stronger than the loyalty to their own country. The socialist, therefore, tends to have an internationalist, as opposed to a nationalist, outlook and loyalty.

It helps if you understand the *reality* of socialism as opposed to theory. The theory says that the people own the means of production. In practice, the state owns it, and whoever controls the state, controls the people and the means of production.

Let's use a public park for an example. The public park in your city is theoretically owned by the public, but you, as a member of that public, cannot decide to sell it or chop down the trees for firewood or even pick the flowers to decorate your home. You cannot plant food for your family in the park which you "own." In short, you do not really own it in any meaningful sense of the word. It is "owned" by the government and the government controls its use.

There was talk during the recent coal strike of our government nationalizing the coal mines. If that had happened, how do you suppose the government would have gone about it? Chances are the government would have purchased the mines from the private owners and then, since the government has no expertise at operating mines, it very likely would have hired these same people to run them. There would have been little financial hardship on the owners, but they would have come under the absolute control of the government.

Until very recently, many people who were socialist would never publicly say so. Socialism has never been popular with the American people and so some socialists decided to follow the democratic-socialist, Fabian idea which originated in England. That idea was simply to advocate socialism on a piecemeal basis while never calling it that. Most of what we refer to as the welfare state is socialism wearing a different name.

In some cases, socialism—and the desire to promote it—motivate members of the Establishment. In other cases, however, I think the motivation is simply greed. Some of the large international banks headquartered in our country have made massive loans to Communist countries, including the Soviet Union. It is estimated that the total Communist debt to western institutions is around $40 billion.

When a bank makes a relatively small loan to an individual or a business, the bank has considerable power over the individual or the business. It can repossess the collateral and cut off further credit. On the other hand, if a bank makes too large a loan, then the recipient gains some leverage over the bank, for then it becomes almost as much a disaster for the bank as for the debtor if the debtor defaults.

The situation is even more acute when banks make loans to governments. The bank, really, has no collateral. It cannot repossess a country, and since no bank has its own army, if a debtor government decides to default, there is nothing the bank can do to stop it.

That's why Communist governments in Eastern Europe and the Soviet Union are in a position to pressure the banks which so foolishly lent them such large sums of their depositors' money. Defaulting on these billions of dollars in loans would destroy many of these banks and the bankers know it. This factor, too, may help explain why so many bankers are suddenly interested in detente, in getting along with Communists, and in U.S. aid to the Third World—where they also made bad loans. It also explains why American bankers supported the Panama Canal giveaway.

Furthermore, most of the Establishment is tied directly or indirectly to the large multinational corporations which have assets and business interests all over the globe. A great many writers have shown how the large oil companies have influenced the State Department and U. S. foreign policy. These huge corporations have such diverse interests that many seem to neglect their responsibilities to the American people.

I was shocked to learn that in the 1940s Aramco, a consortium of oil companies, sold oil to Japanese—and at a lower rate than it did to the American Navy. In the 1930's, Standard Oil and General Motors sold I. G. Farben, the Nazi chemical firm, the secrets of the tetraethyl lead process that Hitler needed for his aircraft.

This, too, is a source of pressure for increased trade with Communist countries and for diplomatic relations with Communist Vietnam and Communist China. Right now American firms are building the world's largest truck factory in Russia, a mammoth plant capable of producing more trucks in one year than all of

America's firms combined. When Lenin said the capitalists would sell the Soviets the rope with which to hang them, he underestimated the greed of some of the capitalists. They seem to be falling over each other in the rush to sell rope.

This is nothing new. Recently declassified documents show heavy multinational investments in Nazi Germany. One of the earliest advocates of diplomatic recognition of the Soviet Union was the Rockefeller public relations man, Ivy Lee. In fact, the record of American financial assistance to the Soviet Union dates back to the beginning of the Russian revolution.

It seems clear that we cannot rely on most of the multinational corporations to look out for the best interests of our nation. They have grown so large and so global in scope that even though their chief executives and owners are American, their loyalties seem to be primarily to the corporations. Overcharging the American armed forces, evading our anti-trust laws, exporting production facilities and jobs, and building up the productive capacity of our potential and obvious adversaries are hardly evidence of having American interests at heart.

That is why many Establishment figures have traditionally pushed us toward a world government—first the League of Nations and later the United Nations. The latest word they are using to sell this idea is "interdependence." The amount of propaganda that is being fed to us on the alleged need for interdependence and a new world economic order is staggering.

Let's pause and examine the idea of interdependence. We do indeed need to import materials in order to maintain our defenses and our standard of living. To import, we need to export. America has *always* been interdependent in the sense of trading with the rest of the world. We have never, from the first birthday of our country, been entirely self-sufficient. No nation is. But what propagandists for a world government have done is to extend the idea from trade to political ties.

It is not necessary that we compromise our sovereignty in order to buy coffee beans in Brazil nor is it necessary for Brazil to sacrifice its sovereignty in order to buy heavy equipment from us. Trade can be conducted easily between separate and sovereign states and has been since the first nations were formed.

A world government is just that—a government which enacts laws people must obey and which has the military power to enforce those laws. Given the present state of the world's nations, which are mostly dictatorships, there is no feasible way for us to be part of a world government and continue to provide our people with the blessings of liberty. A world government formed today would be totalitarian and we would become its serfs.

Yet many leaders continue to push the idea. Here are just a few establishment organizations seeking to reduce American sovereignty: The Atlantic Union Committee, Inc.; World Fellowship, Inc.; United World Federalists; the Institute for International Order; and the United States Committee for the U.N.

Ironically, the same figures who are telling us we must heed growing nationalism in the Third World are telling us that we must become internationalist.

What, after all, is a nationalist? He is nothing more than what most of us are, a person whose primary loyalty and concern is for his own country. This does not mean that he is unwilling to trade with other countries or establish diplomatic relations or engage in cultural or social exchanges; it simply means that he looks out first for his own country where, as Jefferson said, his family, his property, and interests are.

The internationalist, on the other hand, is first a bride without a groom. There is no world government. He must seek one and in the desire for one, he confesses that he does not place the well-being of his own country first in his heart. This attitude—internationalism or as it's called today, interdependence—is being pressed on our children in most school systems. A nation which does not teach its children a patriotic love for it will not long survive. These children will become adults who will neither work nor sacrifice to protect and preserve what they do not value or cherish.

Still, why do many of the very rich in our country advocate either a socialist society or believe so fervently that the U.S. and the Soviet Union can be blended into a compatible world government?

We have already seen that socialism does not, in fact, deliver what it promises, that is; a uniform distribution of wealth. The clever and the ruthless rule every socialist country. Socialism and communism are, in fact, just modern fronts for a very old form of government: oligarchy, rule by a few people.

In the Soviet Union today, about 15 per cent of the population rules the remaining 85 per cent. The 15 per cent, or the oligarchy, have special privileges, luxuries, the best jobs. They are not at all unlike the aristocrats who ruled pre-Revolutionary Russia. They are even careful that their children marry the "right" person in order to maintain their privileged position among the Communist Party faithful.

We normally do not think of ourselves as being saddled with an oligarchy, but to an extent we are. Our "oligarchy" is comprised of the Establishment figures we have been talking about, most of them people of immense wealth who are relatively close-knit both socially and financially.

Their power is exercised indirectly but it is there, influencing both government decisions and public opinion. Some of them have, perhaps naturally, come to see themselves as an elite who have the obligation to take care of the masses.

Elitism, and the arrogance it breeds, is a state of mind, a self-conception of superiority, and that is why in the face of history, in the face of public opinion, in defiance of logic, the elitist stubbornly pushes on with his own beliefs intact.

So they persist in their vision that one day, as the U.S. becomes more collectivist, that there can be a convergence, that a possibly more benign future Soviet elite will form a partnership with them and run a world government backed up by our combined military power which will do for the world what they believe is good for them.

When you strip away the altruism, you have an old-fashioned dictatorship of an elite making serfs out of the rest of the people.

Even if the idea of convergence were correct, I would want no part of it, nor would I want to impose such a system on my children and grandchildren. The tragedy is that the *idea* is pathetically out of touch with *reality*. Our elite is an elite of wealth, of people who, however arrogant, are basically decent and well-intentioned. The elite of the Soviet Union is an elite of the toughest, most ruthless, and most vicious—those men who have survived the terrible climb to power by acts of betrayal, murder, deceit, and inhumanity. It is an elite, as one Ukrainian exile described it, "of modern Mongol savages."

The leftists in the American Establishment, if they succeed in their goal, will only have committed suicide. They will learn that at close quarters there is no contest between a Harvard education and a quick trigger finger. They will learn that wealth offers no defense against a bullet and that the quickest way to acquire wealth, in the Soviet view of things, is to shoot the people who own it and then take it.

We plain Americans will have to save the elite because, in forfeiting their own lives, they also will forfeit ours. I cannot leave this subject, though, without cautioning you on one point that is necessary for clear thinking. I have spoken of an elite and an Establishment as forces which are engaged in psychological warfare against the principles of American nationalism and its corollaries, a strong defense and a strategy to defeat communism.

But remember, not every person of great wealth or member of the Establishment advocates appeasement and socialism! Former Secretary of the Treasury William E. Simon, for example, is an investment banker and an Eastern Establishment figure yet there is no stronger advocate of free enterprise and a strong defense than Bill Simon.

Chapter VIII

The U.N. Versus Freedom

The United Nations began as an instrument of peace. It was directed at those values—freedom and human rights—which we hold dear, but one of the most important steps we can take for American survival is to shed our illusions and hopes about the U.N. and look at the organization as it really is—instead of as we might wish it were.

The first point to consider is that dreams cannot be imposed on reality. At least not in the short run. As much as we may not like it, the world has from its beginnings operated on the basis of power—military and economic. No fundamental changes in political relationships between people or nations has ever been effected except by power. Diplomacy without power is like a car without gasoline or a cannon without ammunition. Actually, diplomacy is the direction of power to resolve conflicts.

That's why advocates of a world government have always faced a political dilemma in their respective nations. A world government is no different than a national government. It must have a legislative body to create laws, an executive branch to administer them—and the military power to enforce them.

Obviously, it must be sovereign; that is, it must have both the jurisdiction and the power to rule people. Since people cannot be ruled by two competing sovereigns, world government becomes a reality only at the expense of national governments.

To date, no nation which possessed military and economic power has been willing to surrender that power. The League of Nations, a product of an Anglo-American Establishment, failed because while those who conceived it had great influence, they did not have sufficient influence to persuade the member nations to surrender their power. Thus, rules and ideals were adopted but could not be enforced. The dream of a world in which nations settled their disputes peacefully could not alter the reality of a world of powerful national states ruled by men willing to resort to war.

In fact, the final irony of the idealist's dream of peace through world government is that it can only be achieved by a world government with sufficient military power to wage and win wars.

The United Nations, which began October 24, 1945, while shifting slightly more in the direction of a world government than the old League, still fell short. The General Assembly cannot legislate. The Security Council, which does have the power to commit armed forces to "peacekeeping" missions, is subject to being thwarted by a veto from any of the five permanent members.

Let's assume for a moment that the people who created the United Nations and wrote its charter sincerely believed the words they wrote. Even with this assumption, the U.N. was founded on sand instead of bedrock because the Communist countries which signed the charter had never in the past, did not at the time, have not since, nor will in the future, observe the high ideals of respect for individual rights and nonaggression called for in its articles.

It was as if an Anti-Crime Commission had been formed in which J. Edgar Hoover was one member and Lucky Luciano was the other and each had a veto power to block any action the commission might wish to take.

There is an important principle involved here and that is that in order for two sides to compromise, both sides must share the same fundamental goals. If you and I both agree that the U.S. should have a strong defense, we can reach a compromise on the composition of that defense force. On the other hand, if you believe that the U.S. should have no defense force at all, then a compromise is impossible. If I proposed even a small defense force and you accepted it, that would be a surrender of your position, not a compromise.

One of the reasons we have been losing the war with communism is that the Communists understand this conflict while our leaders have not admitted it. The Communists know that their basic philosophy is a contradiction of our basic philosophy. Contradictions cannot co-exist.

For communism to succeed, capitalism must fail; for Communist nations to prosper, capitalist nations must perish. That is why they have never yielded one inch in either negotiations or actions except when they were forced to do so by military power. They know they are in a war to the death; too many of our leaders have refused to recognize this fact.

So, even assuming all the organizers of the United Nations believed in the idealistic words contained in its original charter, it was from the moment of its inception fatally poisoned by the inclusion of the Communist powers.

Today, only a handful of the 140 nations which are members, practice the principles contained in the U.N. Charter and the U.N. Declaration of Human Rights—and they are under attack, within the U.N., by those members who do not!

I reject, however, the assumption that the framers of the U.N. actually believed the idealistic words which were sold the people of the world. To make such an assumption you have to believe that men who led the nations which fought World War II were naive and they obviously were not.

If you read the preamble to the U.N. Charter, you can see that it was never intended to rule out the use of war. One clause of it reads as follows: " . . .to ensure, by the acceptance of principles and the institution of methods, that armed force shall not be used, *save in the common interest . . .*"

The United Nations was clearly intended to be a postwar extension of the World War II alliance. All the real authority was relegated to the Security Council in which the U.S., Great Britain, China, Russia, and France are permanent members, each possessing a veto power.

Time, however, has destroyed the alliance. Great Britain and France are no longer major powers. Russia was and is Communist and Nationalist China has been replaced by Red China. Of the five original "great powers," only the United States remains both a great power and actively committed to the principles of freedom.

The United Nations, then, was intended to be and has been used as an instrument of policy by the various nations. We used it to go to war in Korea. It is often said it was an accident that the Soviet Union was boycotting the Security Council meetings at the time of the North Korean attack, the implication being that had it been there it would have vetoed U.N. response.

That is a myth. The Soviet Union helped plan the North Korean invasion and certainly knew not only the day but the hour the attack was to take place. If it was absent, it was absent on purpose. The charter provides that all peacekeeping forces shall be under the direction of the secretary-general and his staff. As I mentioned earlier, from 1945 until the present, the under-secretary in charge of security has been from the Soviet bloc. Perhaps that is why they were absent.

In Korea, for the first time, Americans fought and died under the flag and control of a third party. For the first time, we were forced into a no-win posture. For the first time in the history of the Republic, the American armed forces took the field and did not come home victorious.

Since then the U.N. has grown even more anti-U.S. in its composition. U.N. forces were used to crush the rebellion of the province of Kantanga, compelling it to remain in the newly independent Congo, now called Zaire. This was in spite of the fact that the U.N. Charter clearly forbids inteference in a member nation's internal affairs.

That, of course, did not stop the U.N. from pressuring us to give up the Panama Canal, from branding Zionism a form of racism, from setting up arms and trade embargoes against Rhodesia and South Africa. Even the supposedly humanitarian organizations like UNESCO and UNICEF have been perverted to accomplished political goals by the Communists and other zealots who have placed themselves in these bureaucracies.

The U.N. Declaration of Human Rights has become a mockery as member nations commit atrocities and repressions. In Africa especially, the U.N. has applied a hypocritical double-standard, refusing to condemn guerrilla raids against civilians but condemning military actions against the guerrillas. So far from honesty has the U.N. traveled that it can, with a straight face, declare South Africa a threat to world peace in order to justify intervention in that republic's internal affairs.

The United Nations, as it exists in reality, presents two dangers to the American people: 1. the machinery for diluting or surrendering American sovereignty is in place—a constant temptation to the world government zealots in our country; and 2. it totally confuses and disrupts our foreign policy objectives.

Nothing made this more clear than Andrew Young's actions as U.S. ambassador to the United Nations. Quite often it appeared that Young was confused about which country he was supposed to be representing. When other nations arrogantly and openly asserted their national interests, Young frequently joined them in asserting their interests at our expense.

He became virtually a spokesman for the two Soviet-supported guerrilla leaders who murdered over 1,000 civilians in Rhodesia, and attacked the plan worked out by Rhodesian whites and moderate blacks to bring about peaceful black majority rule. One of the guerrilla leaders Young supported openly declares that the only acceptable solution to him is a Marxist dictatorship.

The U.N.'s role as an espionage center is obvious. Time and again Soviet and other Communist personnel attached to the U.N. have been caught engaged in espionage. Communist Cuba has a U.N. delegation almost as large as the Soviet Union's. Many of these people operate under the protection of diplomatic immunity. It is no exaggeration to say that the U.N. has come to be Communist-dominated and a forum from which to abuse the U.S. Few American taxpayers realize that the United States pays a full 25 per cent of all U.N. costs!

The danger to our sovereignty and independence is real. Decisions of the U.N. Security Council are binding on members. We clearly disregarded our own tradition of freedom of speech by shutting down the Rhodesian Information Office in response to a Security Council directive. The hypocrisy of that action is illustrated by the fact that the terrorist Palestine Liberation Organization as well as all of the Communist bloc nations freely conduct their propaganda activities inside the United States.

The International Court, another U.N. organization, has the authority to compel nations to accept its jurisdiction in certain matters. The Connally Reservation, passed by congress, declares that the U.S. shall determine what matters of its own shall fall under the International Court's jurisdiction.

The U.S. State Department, which vigorously opposed the Connally Reservation, is continuously seeking to repeal it. Recently, the State Department, in a report which was accepted by President Jimmy Carter, said, "At an appropriate time, we shall recommend that the senate re-examine the Connally Reservation with a view to its withdrawal and the filing of a new adherence to the compulsory jurisdiction of the court without the reservation." This could mean a definite and dangerous loss of sovereignty.

The liberals in the U.S. Congress are in fact pushing for ways to strengthen the U.N. at the expenses of American national sovereignty. Sen. George McGovern and Sen. Howard Baker co-sponsored legislation which called on the executive branch to conduct a review of ways to strengthen the U.N. Complying with this legislation, President Carter stated, in presenting his proposals in 1978:

"If we are to develop adequate machinery for management of the world's common problems, a central concern of our foreign policy in the remaining years of this century must be the building of a more effective U.N. system. To this end, this administration is committed to working for a stronger and more effective United Nations."

The degree to which internationalism has infected our government in all its branches is no better illustrated than by the incident which took place in Philadelphia on January 30, 1976. There in Congress Hall where the birth of our nation took place with the signing of the Declaration of Independence, a new document, sponsored by the World Affairs Council, was endorsed by eighty representatives and twenty-four senators. It is called "The Declaration of Interdependence."

The signing of this document was the first step in a thirteen-year program to "educate" the American people on the benefits of interdependence. The document, written by Henry Steele Commanger, calls for surrender of sovereignty, international control of the sea and space, redistribution of wealth, and removes science from the service of national defense.

When I first learned of this document, I was shocked and angered. Over a million Americans have given their lives to achieve and maintain the independence of the United States. The idea that congressmen and senators who swear an oath not only to defend but to "bear true faith and allegiance" to the Constitution would trade away U.S. sovereignty is appalling.

Most of these congressmen belong to Members of Congress for Peace Through Law, a lobbying organization within the congress which is dedicated to our disarmament and to a world government. It was founded in 1966, according to the *Congressional Quarterly*, by Sen. George McGovern and former Sen. Joseph Clark after Clark had been approached by Joan McKinney of the staff of the United World Federalists.

Practically all of the damage done by the congress to the security of the United States and to the freedom of anti-Communist nations in recent years can be laid squarely at the door of Members of Congress for Peace Through Law.

The MCPL's China committee pushed for diplomatic recognition of Red China and played a key role in urging President Nixon to take the initiative in that direction which he did. It also worked to abandon the seventeen million free Chinese on Taiwan.

The United Nations Committee of the MCPL is pushing the efforts to strengthen the United Nations, and the East-West Trade Committee of the MCPL is seeking to liberalize trade and credit with Communist countries. The MCPL's Southeast Asia Committee led the way to our abandoning South Vietnam, Laos and Cambodia.

The MCPL led the fight to scuttle the B-1 bomber, to delay development of the MX missile, to block any U.S. intervention in the Soviet takeover of Africa, to delay the cruise missile and the neutron warhead, to give away the Panama Canal, and to accept a SALT II Treaty which freezes our military inferiority.

In reviewing the record of these men and women, it is difficult not to question their sanity, if not their loyalty. They seem bent on a course of national suicide in spite of all the evidence before them.

Senators Frank Church of Idaho and McGovern of South Dakota are now promoting the fortunes of Fidel Castro, even while Cuban troops help subvert African nations. Church and McGovern were instrumental in blocking any further aid to South Vietnam at a time when North Vietnam had launched a massive attack with conventional forces in clear violation of the Paris Peace Agreement. And this pair of senators led the move to bar any effective assistance to pro-western factions in Angola at the very time 15,000 Cuban soldiers armed with Russian weapons were landing in Luanda.

Politicans such as Church and McGovern are out of touch with the desires of the American people and defied the will of the majority of American people on the canal issue. Many of them may be basically decent people. Many of them may serve their constituents well administratively in answering mail and in assisting with problems with the bureaucracy. Many of them may have the best intentions in the world, but they are, today, the most dangerous people in the United States.

We must replace them at the earliest possible moment with men and women who take their oath of office seriously, who are loyal to the tried and proven principles that have made this nation great: independence, military strength, a free economy, and a rational foreign policy based clearly on the national interests of the United States.

Chapter IX

The Stories They Don't Tell

Ours has been called the age of mass media. For many Americans much of their perception of reality is a result of information received from the news media. How powerful that influence is was brought home to me by President Lyndon Johnson, who was an avid television news watcher.

Some of you may recall the Battle of Khe Sanh during the Vietnam War. It had been my decision, with General Westmoreland's approval, to deploy Marines there to block a major advance by North Vietnamese regulars. Before making that decision, I had walked the terrain and made a careful study of the area. I was confident that it was defendable and that we could hold it and that is exactly what happened.

The Marine ground forces with superb support from Air Force and Marine pilots and South Vietnamese soldiers killed over 12,000 North Vietnamese regulars in seventy-seven days of unending combat with the loss of only 205 Marines. It was a crushing defeat for the NVA and stopped two divisions of the North Vietnamese Army which had orders to capture Hue.

As it turned out, I was re-assigned to the United States before the actual battle began so I was able to see the television version of events. The image presented to the American people was that

Khe Sanh was another Dienbienphu, a hopeless siege which must end only in disaster. During that siege, one C-130 aircraft was hit and burned on the landing strip. Every night for a week, I saw that one plane shown from different angles conveying the impression to many viewers that our planes were falling to enemy fire by the dozen.

So pervasive was this impression of Khe Sanh's hopelessness that even President Johnson thought it might be lost. At the time, I was on a short trip with him to El Toro Marine Base in California and he detoured to Palm Springs in order to brief former President Dwight Eisenhower on the war situation. At the time, the battle of Khe Sanh was going full throttle. At the end of the briefing, President Johnson asked me if I would care to predict whether or not the Marines would hold Khe Sanh.

"Yes, sir, our Marines will hold it," I said. After we had left, the president put his arm around my shoulders and said, "General, it took a lot of guts to make such a positive statement like that to two presidents. That's what I admire about you Marines—you've got so damned much faith in your corps, it's almost like a religion with you."

We do have confidence in our Marines, but I also knew what he did not know: that the situation at Khe Sanh being reported by the news media bore only a minimal resemblance to reality. The outcome, contrary to the media picture given to the American people, was never in doubt.

Why was Khe Sanh presented as a doomed outpost? I think to add drama and suspense. On several occasions when I was I Corps commander in Vietnam, I asked television crews why they didn't tell the story of the Marines' Civic Action Program.

We were helping the Vietnamese to build or rebuild hundreds of schools, churches, roads and other public facilities. We helped them plant and harvest their rice. We set up orphanages and medical clinics and helped the people in the area regain their confidence and their pride. It was a heart-warming and humane side of the war.

The answers I got from the television crews were always the same. They did try to tell the story. They shot thousands of feet of film and wrote dozens of stories about the civic action program, but editors back in the States concentrated on the horror and the combat. One CBS cameraman told me that for every hundred minutes of film he took, less than five minutes of it ever made the TV screen and it was always the most dramatic and bloody part—and was quite often out of context.

One more story will illustrate the problem. In 1968, the North Vietnamese made a blunder. It became known as the Tet Offensive. They made a massive attempt to assault the principal cities of South Vietnam and they suffered staggering losses without achieving their objectives. After the battles were over, Walter Cronkite, the CBS anchor man, came to South Vietnam for an on-the-spot report. A Marine lieutenant colonel was provided to take him on a tour of Hue, which had been a scene of heavy fighting.

At that time, the city was completely cleared. There was no fighting going on at all. I was stunned, therefore, when I saw Cronkite on television, standing in Hue, microphone in hand, while in the background were the sounds of machine gun fire and explosions, which apparently had been dubbed in by sound effects men.

The Tet Offensive, which was both a strategic blunder and a military disaster for the North Vietnamese, was reported to the American people as a defeat for our forces and those of South Vietnam.

Peter Braestrup, formerly of the *Washington Post* and one of the most perceptive and honest newsmen who reported the war, did a study of the media coverage of the Tet Offensive and came to the same conclusion. He has been rewarded for his efforts with ridicule.

Dr. Ernest Lefever, a research fellow at the Brookings Institute, did an analysis of CBS Television's news in 1972 and 1973. The results of his study were published under the title, *TV and National Defense*, by the Institute for American Strategy.

At one point in his book, Dr. Lefever writes: "CBS Evening News, as demonstrated in Chapter 5, was highly critical of the U.S. position on Vietnam. . . . CBS newsmen advocated a speedy withdrawal with little regard for what happened to South Vietnam and deplored the U.S. bombings of military targets in the North. CBS Evening News promoted this perspective by direct expressions of opinion from its own newsmen, by quoting others, and by the selection of news which was heavily critical of the Saigon government, while tending to apologize for or even to glamorize the Hanoi regime. There was a constant barrage of criticism against the U.S. military, not only in Vietnam, but across the board.''

In another part of the book, Dr. Lefever analyses CBS coverage of U.S. military affairs in 1972 and 1973, classifying for each year a number of different stories. In 1972, for example, CBS devoted 23 minutes and 10 seconds of air time to racial discrimination and riots in the military; one minute to the U.S.-USSR military balance. In 1973, CBS devoted 33 minutes of air time to corruption and misconduct in the military and zero time to the U.S.-USSR military balance.

The question that comes to mind when you review studies such as these or reflect on your own experiences with biased or unbalanced reporting, is why? To answer that, we have to look at the nature of the news business. There is no one answer, but several.

First, news is what people in the news business say is news. We consumers of news have been conditioned to think that news includes everything which has happened of any importance. Implicit in this false assumption is the equally false assumption that if it is not reported as news, it is not important.

In other words, people inside the news business make personal judgments as to which events they will present to their public. The criteria which go into these judgments are not, as most people believe, strictly relative to the importance of the event, but include such factors as drama and entertainment value as well.

Second, each medium, whether it's television, newspapers, or magazines, has inherent physical limitations which force newsmen to make selective judgments. There is only so much time, only so many column inches of space per issue. No medium can ever tell us everything it has available to tell on any given day. Choices have to be made and one of the criteria for making the choices is entertainment value as well as any "need to know."

In addition there is the limitation imposed by the quality of the people employed—their maturity, their intelligence, their education, their experience. Since the news business from start to finish is a business involving the continuous exercise of personal judgment, the qualities of the people making the judgments are very important indeed in the determining of the final product.

This factor played a large role in the generally poor coverage of the Vietnam War. In previous wars, correspondents assigned to cover them were for the most part the very top people in their profession—people who could view the sad tragedy of war but keep their perspective. In Vietnam, anyone who could produce a letter from any publication or other outlet promising to use their material became an "accredited war correspondent." I was appalled to see the parade of housewives, young girls, retired military people out for a last whiff of gunsmoke, and other obviously amateur reporters who came to report one of the most complex wars in our history. And so were many of the very fine and experienced war correspondents.

My favorite example is a young reporter who showed up for the initial briefing in Saigon given to all new arrivals to acquaint them with the country and the situation on the battlefield. The young officer giving the briefing was explaining at one point about the deployment of some infantry battalions.

The newly arrived reporter raised his hand. "Could you tell me what a battalion is?"

The briefing officer was stunned. "Ye Gods, mister! Didn't you prepare yourself in any way before you came all the way out here?"

"Oh, no," the young reporter said. "My editor told me he wanted me to come over here with an open mind."

Finally there is a third factor that contributes to the present state of the press in the U.S. and that is the growing concentration of ownership. There are about 1,700 daily newspapers in the U.S. but only a fraction have their own correspondents in Washington. And many of those instruct their Washington people to concentrate only on news affecting their home areas.

For national news, the bulk of the newspapers and radio stations rely on two wire services, United Press International and the Associated Press. Thus, it's no exaggeration to say that the majority of our newspaper and radio stations rely on the judgments of two people, the Washington bureau chiefs of the AP and the UPI, for most of their national news.

There are only three major television networks—ABC, CBS, and NBC—and all three have their major operations located in New York City and Washington, D.C. Virtually all of the independent television stations rely on one of these three networks for their national and international news.

A news organization is like any other. Somewhere in the organization, one person has to have the final responsibility for making decisions. Thus, a handful of human beings each day have the final say on what 99 per cent of the American people will see as national and international news on their television sets.

There are only three newspapers that can be considered national newspapers. One of these, the *Wall Street Journal*, is essentially a business newspaper. The other two are the *New York Times*, and the *Washington Post*, and both exert enormous influence, not only on their readers, but on other newsmen.

So when you analyse the situation, there is a relatively small number of individuals—most of them unknown to the general public—who control the daily flow of news to the country as a whole. They all live and work in only two cities, New York and Washington. This is not the result of any conspiracy nor am I suggesting that these people in any way set out to deceive the American people. The concentration is simply the result of the way the news business has physically evolved in the U.S.

But there is a problem. So few decision-makers concentrated in one region make the likelihood of conformity in thought much greater. What the *New York Times* views as important or unimportant, the *Post*, the networks, and the wire services are likely also to view as important or unimportant. At the same time the others have some influence on the *Times*.

As Alexander Solzhenitsyn said in his Harvard speech in 1978, news becomes what is fashionable. I believe this is the process that is reflected by Dr. Lefever's study, rather than a conscious decision to distort the war. The war simply became unfashionable. Peer pressure reinforced and confirmed the notion. "Everybody" thought the same thing. Thus each decision-maker's judgment was confirmed by his competitor's.

But whether these people wish it or not, they hold in their hands enormous power. By exercising their individual judgments, as they are paid to do, they not only serve their own interests, but actually determine what shall and what shall not become of public interest.

I and others, including over seventy congressmen, attempted to warn the American public in 1971 that all the trends pointed toward the fact that the Soviet Union was achieving military superiority, but the collective judgments of the key news media people were that such a warning was not news. As Lefever's study of the video tapes revealed, in two full years of broadcasting, CBS devoted sixty seconds to reporting the U.S.-Soviet military balance. For all the people who heard those of us who were speaking out, we might as well have been standing on an apple box in the middle of the Gobi desert.

Abraham Lincoln said in 1858, "With public sentiment, nothing can fail; without it, nothing can succeed. Consequently, he who molds public sentiment goes deeper than he who enacts statutes or pronounces decisions. He makes statutes and decisions possible or impossible to be executed."

Charles W. Bray, press spokesman for the State Department from 1971 to 1973, said the same thing: "To an extraordinary degree, television and newspapers set the national agenda: by their treatment or nontreatment of issues, they define what is important and, hence, what gets decided and acted upon in our government."

I believe that many members of the press have not fully realized this enormous public power they possess. Many of them, as they perform their jobs, are thinking in terms of meeting the requirements of their job, not in terms of what effect their work has on the nation in general. They are judging events subjectively from a standpoint of "newsworthiness," not from the standpoint of whether you or I should know about a particular event.

I have always had great respect and admiration for the members of the press who do a difficult job well and I am one of those who would rather have a free press, warts and all, than a controlled press. Furthermore, I have faith that the American press will, as it comes to grips with its enormous power, correct its obvious faults and better serve the public interest.

I will never forget the words of a North Vietnamese major who surrendered to our forces in April, 1966, at Danang. We had a long conversation and at one point he said the North Vietnamese had given up any hope of winning on the battlefield but believed that if they kept the war going on long enough, they could win it in the political and psychological arenas of America.

Americans are naive, Major Thang said, and do not realize what is happening to them. He said guns, tanks, airplanes and soldiers ". . . are as nothing compared to the propaganda guns being used against the people in the United States." He said newspapers, radios, magazines, and television are all "instruments of war," and the Communists are experts at using them.

Subsequent events proved him correct. North Vietnam did win its war in the United States. The *Post*, the *Times*, the television networks proved to be more lethal to the American forces than any of the Russian or Chinese weaponry.

I think the people at these institutions to this day still do not understand what they contributed and how they were exploited. They have not yet come to grips with the new level of sophistication in psychological warfare. They believe they are merely reporting what is happening, but in many cases, they are creating "what is happening."

Political street demonstrations, for example, are today created to be media events. Without prominent coverage and exposure, their effect on public opinion would be insignificant. The lengths to which political zealots will go to get media coverage is illustrated by those in Vietnam who set themselves on fire to protest the Saigon government. The American public is unaware that those suicides were carefully scheduled to make American press deadlines and that the press was notified in advance.

I do not envy those who occupy positions of responsibility in the media. Never before have their responsibilities been greater or their judgments more difficult. In a democracy, there must be a free and open debate of all the issues. If the major media, for whatever reason, intentionally or unintentionally, limit both the issues to be debated and the parameters of the debate, then they short-circuit the democratic process.

On the other hand, as never before, there are cold and calculating people who are both knowledgeable and sophisticated standing ready to exploit the press for political reasons.

Quite clearly, one crucial part of the battle for American survival is being fought daily in the offices of the nation's press.

Chapter X

At the Brink

During the Cape Glouster Battle on New Britain Island in the South Pacific in World War II, "Chesty" Puller, one of the greatest Marines I ever knew, and I chanced to be sharing the protection offered by the rib-like roots of a banyan tree.

It was heavy jungle and we were receiving machine gun and rifle fire from well-entrenched Japanese soldiers. It was one of those times when it seemed that Chesty and I could not get close enough to Mother Earth and the roots of that banyan tree.

During a burst of machine gun fire, I felt a sharp and painful blow on my lower spine. I was momentarily stunned and unable to move. Chesty examined me and found a red swelling lump on my spine which later developed into a black and blue spot two inches in diameter. I was not seriously injured. A spent machine gun bullet lay on the ground. I was very grateful the banyan tree root was three inches thick instead of two; otherwise, the bullet would have severed my spinal cord and I would have known a drastically different future.

Every man or woman who has been in combat can tell similar experiences for nowhere but in battle is the uncertainty of the future more dramatically obvious.

In truth, though, even in peace and even as civilians we face an uncertain future. It's so easy to believe otherwise. We plan our lives, most of us, to some degree and we have the past to reassure us. Last year we planned to do this or that and we did it. We anticipated certain events, like holidays or vacations or birthdays, and they all came to pass. Yet, a little reflection will remind us that life contains no guarantees and that the future is always in a state of flux, actually in the process of being shaped by the present. At best, we live on a contingency basis: we will do this next week if such and such occurs this week. This element of uncertainty is reflected in the folk wisdom of many cultures, from the Southerner who says, "I'll see you next week if the creek don't rise," to the Arab who adds, "If Allah wills."

Our future, as Americans alive in the latter part of the 20th Century, can take several shapes, depending upon what is done today. One way to predict what shape it will take with reasonable accuracy is to extend the trends of the present situation and developments into the future. Suppose, for example, we as a people do nothing in the next year or two to change the present situation in regard to defense and strategy. What will the future hold?

One strong possibility may be nuclear war. Wars have often started on the basis of miscalculations by one party or the other. The Soviet Union might be so encouraged by our military weakness that it might threaten directly some area of our vital interests and thus provoke a direct challenge from an American president. This is what happened in Korea in 1950 and again in 1962 when the Soviets introduced missiles into Cuba. For a few tense hours, the world tottered on the brink of a nuclear exchange. It did so again in 1973, when the Soviets mobilized airborne divisions to intervene in the Yom Kippur War and President Nixon responded with a full military alert.

You would think something so awesome as a world war could not be launched by creatures so frail, so egotistical, so subject to emotions, as men, but all nations, no matter how powerful, are led by ordinary human beings. No magic formula has yet been found to insure that a leader's qualities match his responsibilities.

There is no reason to review the horrors such a war would bring. Science fiction writers have depicted it for decades. What it would mean to mankind, I don't know, but I do know that for nearly all Americans it would mean either death or existence on an animal-like level. A continuation of the present military trends, with us growing weaker and the Soviets growing stronger, will increase the odds of such a war tremendously.

Weakness breeds war. Wars come when an aggressor perceives his potential enemy as psychologically and militarily weak. Linebackers and prize fighters never get mugged.

Our present weakness, if not altered, could bring a different but almost equally tragic future. As we discussed earlier, we are both an "island" nation and a continental nation. We depend heavily on imports for much of our industry. We have all heard the phrase "chain reaction" used to tell what happens inside an atomic reactor. Well, world affairs is really a chain reaction of causes and effects. Suppose, because we are weak militarily, a Marxist regime takes over control of Southern Africa. They might declare an embargo of their strategic minerals and refuse to sell them to us.

Even in a weak state, we might have sufficient conventional military power to seize these countries, but then suppose the Soviet Union says that if we make the attempt, it means war. Then, because of strategic weakness, we would have to back down. The loss of those minerals would eventually shut down many of our industries and Americans would be thrown out of work. Because millions would be out of work and limited in what they could buy, other industries not directly dependent on those minerals would be forced to cut back. Tax revenues would fall, and our economy would slump.

A similar situation could happen with oil. About 47 per cent of our oil is imported. In our weakened military state, we might not be able to prevent unfriendly governments from taking over control of the oil producing states. The allegiance of those in power today can be questioned, but suppose even more hostile people were in control, once again backed up by military might of the Soviet Union. Our oil imports could be reduced to a dribble and our economy would grind to a shadow of its normal strength.

Really massive unemployment, such as these events would produce, would create economic turmoil which domestic radicals would be ready to exploit. We know already that our police departments have difficulty controlling crime in times of relative affluence. With poverty even worse than that produced by the Great Depression, with power plants shutting down or rationing electricity, with our individual mobility reduced because of scarce and surely rationed gasoline, many of our cities, I fear, would explode with violence. The Armed Forces would be called on to restore order and the potential for revolution or coup would be seriously enhanced. People prefer almost anything to chaos. The situation would be greatly aggravated by the total unpreparedness of our National Guard and Army Reserve forces today.

Just imagine for a moment your own situation. Suppose you were laid off and couldn't find a job. There would be some meager government relief, but not enough to buy food and to meet your mortgage payments. Eventually, you would be evicted. Where would you and your family live? There might not even be enough gasoline available to travel any great distance to the homes of relatives if they were any better off. What would you do when your children got hungry or if members of your family were ill and there were no hospital facilities?

Most Americans, thank God, have never been faced with such emergencies and have not had to answer these questions; but I have been in areas of the world where they are asked and I can tell you that when life is reduced to basic survival, interest in what kind of government one has evaporates. Food is the foundation on which civilizations are built and hunger is one of the most basic motivations of man. Take food away and all else will crumble.

Our food supply is almost entirely dependent on oil, for our agriculture is mechanized, from the growing process to the final delivery to the consumer. There are no great reserves of food anymore. New York City, for example, normally has no more than a few days supply in its warehouses. Ironically, our very affluence has made us a vulnerable nation. If we cannot keep the sea lanes open and project our power abroad to the countries where it is needed, we as a nation will soon be brought to our knees.

If you get nothing else from this book except the understanding of the direct cause-and-effect relationships that exist between military power, foreign policy, and domestic well-being, you will have a far better grasp of the dangers facing us than most Americans, including many in responsible government positions.

Without a base of superior military power supporting them, our diplomats cannot exert effective political influence; without credible influence in many foreign nations, we cannot guarantee the flow of vital metals and minerals on which our economy depends. Without that flow of metals and minerals, our sophisticated economy cannot function; and without our economy functioning, we cannot eat.

I am not a defeatist. I believe we can build a better future. What would the future hold if we returned to the tradition of a strong and invincible America? If we rebuilt our strategic forces (and we have the ability to do it if we have the will) to the point there would be no question of who would win a nuclear war, there would very likely never be one.

With a credible base of strategic power, so that in a showdown an American president could force the Soviet Union to back away, our conventional forces—if rebuilt to the necessary strength—could easily keep open the sea lanes and project our power wherever it was needed. With this military power behind them, our diplomats could effectively negotiate and maintain fair and good relations with other nations whose trade is vital to our well-being.

Behind a shield of military strength and with a free flow of trade, the American economy can continue to generate the jobs and healthy economy necessary to alleviate domestic problems. With a well-fed and working nation, we can maintain and foster the great experiment in human liberty our forefathers began in 1776.

Time works against, and pressures the Soviet Union. Its socialist slave labor economy is a failure. Its satellite nations are held by armed force and grow increasingly restless. We know from Soviet dissidents that even in Russia proper the promises of communism have been found wanting and the new generations are cynical about the dictatorial bureaucracy which dominates their lives.

There is good reason to believe that if we maintain our strength and apply pressure through diplomatic and economic channels on the Soviet Union, that the power-hungry totalitarians could be replaced by a more rational and moral leadership. Hundreds of millions of people, held captive by the Communists, are praying that we will have the strength of spirit and determination to finish the course and thus, by our own survival, insure their eventual liberation.

Regardless of what direction future Soviet leaders take or what policies develop in the Third World, the United States can remain both free and prosperous so long as we maintain our military and economic power.

If you will take your choice of any history book and start with ancient Egypt and read on into modern times, you will see that no great nation has ever existed any longer than the supremacy of its military power. When the military power of Athens declined, the Golden Age of Greece came to an abrupt halt. Carthage fell to Rome, and when Rome became too weak militarily, the closest thing to world government the West has ever seen collapsed before a military onslaught. In each case, the decline of military power resulted from moral decay and lack of will on the part of the people and their leaders.

The great artists of the Renaissance painted while under the protection of military power. The philosophy and ideas of self-government in England were nourished behind the shield of the British Navy. Indeed, up until World War II, the United States relied greatly on the protective influence and capability of the British Navy. No nation has ever survived without the protection of military power, whether its own or its allies. Even tiny Switzerland, the classic neutral, has a strong defense force made up by universal military training which extends into middle age for all able-bodied males. Swiss reservists keep weapons and ammunition in their homes. They know that to live in peace you must be ready and able to fight in a war.

That is the way the world is because that is the way human nature is and wishing it weren't so won't change it. I've seen too much of the realities of war to believe any romantic notions about it. I fervently hope my grandchildren will never have to endure its hell. But they must be conscious of the threat and prepared for it, nevertheless. Real peace and freedom can only be achieved and maintained through strength and those who tell you otherwise are speaking from ignorance—or intentionally misleading you.

The future of our United States—of you and me—is being molded today. If we are to avoid the grim, dark future of war and defeat or of economic strangulation with the same results, we must act today to restore our military power to its former supremacy. That is the price of a safe, peaceful and prosperous future. We must pay it or pay the much heavier price of poverty, destruction, and slavery.

Our military strength did not decline by accident, nor did our diplomacy take the road of retreat by necessity. Both situations are a direct result of conscious but erroneous decisions made by specific individual human beings. If we are to change the effects, we must change the cause—and put new, dedicated and realistic people into positions of leadership.

Chapter XI

Ten Steps Toward Security

Some people occupying positions of leadership in our country today are like the Roman politician standing in the shadows of his balcony, watching a crowd of people hurrying down the street below him.

He turns to his attendant and says, "I must find out where they are going because I am their leader."

Some members of our congress today are demonstrating characteristics of followers rather than leaders. They worry more about getting re-elected than about the security of our nation. They worry more about being a good guy on Capitol Hill or a member of the most fashionable clubs than about their responsibilities to their constituents and to their country.

Some of them are overly influenced by their sense of power, by prestige and by the game of political payoffs and horse trading. They lack dedication, moral courage, in some cases even patriotism, and often show no appreciation of the perils our nation faces. In congress as in all other walks of life, there is no substitute for loyalty, dedication, and hard work if the job is to be done right.

I have witnessed the ultimate sacrifice of thousands of young Americans on the battlefield and I believe that our political leaders

owe us no less loyalty, dedication, and willingness to make sacrifices for the defense of our freedom and our Republic. There are
some members of the congress who meet these criteria but today
they are in the minority.

As a result of this massive abdication of leadership, the American people have not been told the truth about the magnitude and
nature of the dangers facing us, nor have they been provided with
a strategy for survival.

As we pointed out earlier, a team committed only to defensive
reactions is foredoomed. Our leaders have disguised their lack of
strategy by talking endlessly about peace as a goal. Peace is what
we all want, but as an objective for determining strategy it doesn't
work. Peace is too vague a word. The dead are at peace. There
is peace in a prison camp. Peace came to Hungary in 1956 and
to Czechoslavakia in 1968. There is peace in Cambodia. If by
peace, we mean the absence of war or threat of war, we can
achieve that tomorrow by signing a treaty of surrender with the
Soviet Union.

Given such a vague, ill-defined and emotionally-charged national objective as peace, is it any wonder that we are confused
as to what strategy we should adopt to obtain it? But suppose we
define our national goals in more specific terms. Suppose we agree
that as a nation, our objectives are: 1. to remain independent; 2.
to remain prosperous; and 3. to avoid defeat in war or surrender
to nuclear blackmail.

Now we can begin to think more clearly. We now know where
it is we want to go. We can now more clearly determine who
wishes to go with us and who wishes to go in another direction.
We now have a rational basis on which to form a consensus as to
what our strategy for survival should be.

I believe there are ten elements that are essential to our survival
in the present world. If we can accomplish these ten steps, then
we can realize our national objectives of independence, prosperity,
and safety. I hope you will consider these and help us achieve
them. In the last chapter we will discuss ways in which you can
do this.

1. Regain strategic military superiority. Achieving this step will assure us that we will not fall to nuclear blackmail nor tempt our enemies to launch a surprise attack. To achieve this goal, it will be necessary to rearrange our national priorities so that we can build a weapons system that is invulnerable to nuclear attack.

We already have one key component ready for production. That is the B-1 bomber. We must elect a sufficient number of congressmen to revive this project and get the B-1s into the hands of our Air Force. At the same time, we must speed up production of the cruise missile, the neutron warhead, and the Trident submarine. We must also proceed with the rapid development and deployment of a mobile missile system.

Most importantly, we must not allow our present leaders who have blundered us into peril to destroy any hope of recovery by foolishly adopting a strategic arms limitation treaty which will freeze our inferiority. Past experience should teach us two lessons: 1. we cannot trust the Soviet Union to abide by any treaty; and 2. the people who preach SALT are the same ones who preached unilateral disarmament and mutual assured destruction. They were wrong in their assessment of Soviet intentions in the past and they are just as wrong in their assessments today.

2. Build a strong combination of strategic defenses. We must scrap the insane concept of mutual assured destruction which has undermined our defenses. For offensive weapons to register in the enemy's mind as a believable deterrent, defense forces must be strong enough to guarantee that we can survive a nuclear exchange and remain a powerful nation.

We have the technology; we have lacked the will and common sense. This program must be done on a priority basis. We must re-establish a strong air defense against bombers. We must proceed full steam ahead to develop a high-energy beam defensive weapon against missiles. We must simultaneously provide a civil defense program that consists of public education, planned evacuation procedures, and shelters. We must encourage private industry to participate and to provide shelters for their key personnel and blast protection for their machinery.

3. Regain technological and manpower superiority in conventional war capability. Without credible conventional military power, we can easily fall prey to the proven Communist strategy of taking over the world one country at a time—never making a move that would justify all-out war.

We must have the naval capability to keep the sea lanes open and the flow of vital minerals and metals uninterrupted. We must scrap the all-volunteer army concept, too. It is a failure pure and simple. As we pointed out earlier, the alternative should not be a return to the previously unfair draft, but a fair and truly universal conscription plan. Every American shares equally the blessings of liberty; every American should share equally the cost of maintaining it.

4. Restore our security and intelligence-gathering capability. The functions assigned to Defense Intelligence, the Central Intelligence Agency, and the National Security Agency are the eyes and ears of our government. We are blind and deaf without them. We must face the reality that in a hostile world we have no choice in this matter. Recent, misguided efforts to achieve accountability have virtually destroyed the capabilities of our intelligence agencies. We should achieve accountability, but in different ways.

One way is to conduct the audits advocated by Gen. George Keegan, retired head of Air Force Intelligence. General Keegan contends that those who have the responsibility for making assessments and estimates of Soviet capability and intentions have failed miserably. An audit would pinpoint those responsible so we can get them out before they lead us astray again.

Another way is to make the president solely responsible for the failures and successes of the intelligence agencies. Let the congress oversee the president. That way we can avoid the insanity of attempting to conduct secret operations which are under review by congressional committees world-famous for leaking information.

Internal security is the proper job of the FBI and the congress should give it a new mandate, the authority, the funds, and the personnel necessary to sweep our domestic areas clean of Soviet subversion. Re-establishing the internal security committees of the congress might help focus attention on this problem.

5. Stop the flow of technology and credit to the Communist powers. Providing credit and technology and food to the Soviet bloc is probably the greatest single mistake we have made—and for the basest of motives, greed.

No less a person than Alexander Solzhenitsyn has begged us to stop this madness. Speaking of the Russian people who are attempting to resist Communist tyranny, Solzhenitsyn cried out to the West, "They are burying us alive and you are selling them the shovels!"

Cutting off this technology, credit, and food, is the single most damaging blow we can strike short of military action. It will force the Soviet dictators to divert resources away from armaments. Legislation can stop it and this must be one of our goals. There are already laws on the books which govern trade with hostile states, but there are loopholes large enough to admit the latest computers and the world's largest truck factory. The law must be simple and nondiscretionary: no trade, no credit until such time as the Soviet Union opens its borders to the free flow of people and information.

The Soviet Union needs our technology; we do not need their raw materials or finished products made by slave labor. Our new law must contain a provision to punish multinational corporations headquartered in the U.S. if they attempt to trade through their foreign subsidiaries.

6. Establish an honest foreign policy based openly on the national interests of the American people. We must reduce the influence big business has had on the Executive Branch of our government.

We have long held as one of our cardinal principles the separation of church and state. That principle was adopted because our forefathers in their wisdom saw how the intertwining of church and state had brought misery to the people of Europe. We must adopt as an equally firm principle the separation of business and state.

The history of this century provides ample evidence of how the intertwining of business and government can result in human misery. It is not the business of the American government to negotiate business concessions for private interests with foreign governments, nor to protect those private interests with Marines.

A great deal of the hostility people in other lands feel toward our nation is precisely because of the activities of some multinational corporations. Furthermore we have already seen that some of these corporations place their private interests ahead of our national interests.

If an American firm wishes to operate overseas, let it operate at its own risk on whatever terms it can come to with its foreign hosts. We should make it clear that our government's relations with a foreign government will not be influenced one way or the other by how that foreign government treats a private corporation.

Only by reducing the influence of international organizations, both public and private, can we arrive at a foreign policy that the American people will understand, respect and support.

7. Disengage from the United Nations and other world organizations. The United Nations, as we have seen, has become a hostile organization which not only no longer serves our national interests but actively works against them. I believe we would have dealt with, won and terminated the wars in Vietnam and Korea with dispatch had we not been shackled by the United Nations.

Our absence from the United Nations will in no way harm our interests. It may even help bring some of the Third World nations to their senses for the U.N. seems to give some of these nations delusions of grandeur when in fact they are bankrupt and existing on charity. From Fiscal Year 1948 through Fiscal Year 1976, we have pumped over $27 billion into the United Nations, its subsidiary organizations and other world organizations. For that, we have received abuse, scorn, and treachery. Whatever we wish to do in the way of solving world problems, we can do without the United Nations. Once free of this burden, we can establish our strength, reaffirm our leadership of the shrinking Free World, and work in a true partnership with those nations which choose to work with us in a fair and responsible manner. Never again must we allow an American life to be sacrificed on the battlefield under the blue flag of the U.N.

8. Amend the Constitution to forbid deficit spending except in time of national emergency declared by two-thirds vote of both houses of congress. We have seen and are seeing the ravages caused by an inflated currency and how deficit spending contributes to this disease which, if not cured, will destroy us as surely as a nuclear attack. We, the people, must impose this constitutional restraint on our politicians because they have demonstrated in the past that they will act irresponsibly.

9. Strengthen the independence of state and local governments. The principle which our forefathers built into our system to guard us against tyranny was dispersion and separation of powers. They wisely feared too strong a central government and so they were careful to delegate to the central government only certain powers and to specifically reserve all other powers and rights, not so specified, to the states and to the people.

This very vital principle we have abandoned as Washington has assumed a greater and greater role in every American's life. The danger is exactly as our forefathers outlined. An all-powerful central government in the clutches of the wrong people can become a tyrant. It must be one of our goals to seek true decentralization and to return to the states and the people the powers that are rightfully theirs.

This will take a great deal of doing. In some cases, we must seek the repeal of legislation, such as revenue sharing, which is corrupting the independence of local officials. With federal funds has come federal control. Both must be stopped. In other instances, we must seek legislation, which the Constitution authorizes, to limit the jurisdiction of the federal courts where a great deal of federal usurpation of state powers has taken place.

I am not advocating a return to the 19th Century or to the abuses which took place in those years, but rather the need to reestablish a proper balance before state lines become meaningless and we find ourselves being governed in everything we do by federal administrators who are unelected and unanswerable and unresponsive to the people.

It's strange indeed that some of those who advocate a pluralistic world in order to justify appeasing the Soviet Union are dead set against pluralism and diversity in their own country!

10. Re-establish our spiritual strength. This last step must be taken by each individual. Communism is essentially a religion without God. It has its own catechism, its own prophets, its own promise of heaven on earth and it demands of its followers faith and conviction. Effective action is impossible without conviction.

One of the paradoxes in the world today is that the leaders of the free world have lost their faith, not only in God, but in themselves, in their country and in its principles. Thus atheistic communism advances with religious fervor while the free world retreats in cynical despair. We must cast away these leaders who no longer believe we are capable of meeting and overcoming the challenge of communism.

I shall not try to impose my religious beliefs on you, but I do offer this for your consideration. We feel about our nation the way we feel about ourselves. No matter how sophisticated our arguments may be, deep down we do not feel good about ourselves when we are dishonest, unfaithful to our word, lazy, or self-indulgent.

We cannot escape the knowledge imbedded in our subconscious of what a man or woman should and could be: honest in word and deed, dedicated, industrious, disciplined, and brave. This image of virtue is the heritage of mankind and is present in both Western and Eastern cultures.

We do not need God to remind us when we fall short because our consciences, no matter how battered, will do that. There is no such thing as a spiritual rebirth of a nation; there can only be a spiritual rebirth of the individuals who make up a nation. This is one goal that we can begin to work toward in our own hearts at this very moment.

Well, there is a strategy for survival. Some parts of it will be expensive. Some parts may strike many people as too radical. The fact is, our ship of state is sinking fast and radical and expensive actions are necessary to save her.

There are no free rides in the real world. We are going to pay a price. The question is which one: the price of real peace and freedom or the price of doing nothing, which is death and slavery.

Chapter XII

Will We Survive?

Imagine you are driving up a steep, narrow mountain road and suddenly you round a curve and there, blocking your path, is a boulder. There are three different methods you might use to remove that boulder. If you had the right kind of vehicle, you might physically push it out of the way. If you had the time, you might call the nearest highway department and ask them to remove it. If you had enough money, you might hire several strong men to move it for you. Your objective throughout would have been the same—to remove the boulder.

The three alternatives I just outlined to you are examples of three fundamental kinds of power. Power is simply the ability to make something happen—in our example, move the boulder. Sometimes physical power, or force, can be used. Sometimes political power—turning to government—can do the job. And sometimes there is money power, meaning money can be used to make things happen.

If we are to achieve the goals we outlined in the preceding chapter, we will have to utilize some kind of power—some ability to make things happen. If we find that we lack power, then nothing will happen—at least nothing that we want to happen.

As you read your daily newspaper or watch the news on television, you may easily fall into the trap of thinking that things just happen of themselves. The language of the news business encourages this belief. There is a lot of talk about *trends, social forces,* and other abstractions like *nation* and *government* and *economy.* If we are not careful, we begin to think of these things as disembodied entities with the power to act on their own.

But if we pause and think, we remember that institutions have no life of their own. At the controls of every institution are individual human beings just like you and me. The actions of the institutions are the direct result of the decisions made by the human beings.

You probably remember the wonderful movie, *The Wizard of Oz.* When Dorothy and her friends first arrived at the Emerald City and visited the awesome Wizard of Oz, they saw this gigantic disembodied image which spoke with a voice like thunder.

Later they discovered that it was only an image and that hidden behind the curtain was a flesh and blood and quite ordinary old man. So you will find that whether you are talking about world communism or The West or democracies or the Third World or whatever, behind the curtains of each and every one are ordinary human beings.

It is a good rule of thumb to remember that in human affairs, little of great importance happens by accident. Inflation is not a result of forces and trends; it is the direct result of decisions made by human beings who have sat or sit on the Federal Reserve Board, in the White House, and in the Congress. Similarly, the decline of America's military power is neither an accident nor a mystery. Again, it is the direct result of specific decisions made by specific individuals who have sat or sit in the White House, the Congress, and the State and Defense Departments.

So, too, is foreign policy a result of decisions made by people. "It" is not an "it" and "it" does not "evolve." Foreign policy consists of nothing more than a set of decisions made by people to do certain things and to refrain from doing certain other things. Neither monetary nor military nor foreign policy is fixed and unchangeable. Any or all can be changed simply by making new decisions.

This is a most important point. So many people are fooled by the trappings of power and government that they forget that these are human institutions operated by human beings.

A friend of mine once described congressmen as common people with uncommon responsibilities. The same definition applies to generals, admirals, commissars, secretaries of state, presidents, and billionaires.

We can now see that the things we don't like—our military weakness, our constant edging toward world government, our inflationary economy, and our confused foreign policy—are effects caused by the decisions of specific individuals.

Since that is so, and it is so, then to change those things, we must perform one of two actions: 1. either influence the people already in positions of authority to make new decision and/or 2. replace those people with other people who will make new decisions. And since doing either involves the ability to make things happen, we are right back where we started: facing the question of power.

I don't think anyone will argue that the Establishment people who have been making most of these decisions since 1945, or at least influencing the people who did, have immense money power.

If we look at these people, we find they fall into one of two categories. In one category are the actual scions of wealth like David and Nelson Rockefeller, Walt Wriston, Henry Peterson, Averell Harriman and Douglas Dillon. In the second are the servants—in a manner of speaking: academics like Kissinger and Brezinski who have patrons, or Wall Street lawyers like Cyrus Vance, or politicians like President Carter and Senator Frank Church.

I must caution you again to remember we are using the word, "Establishment," in a general sense to describe that group of people who have largely dominated foreign policy thinking in our government. Not all of them are from the East nor do all wealthy people in the East share the same beliefs or support the same policies. I hasten to add, too, that there is nothing illegal or especially sinister about their influence. They are, after all, merely doing what we would like to do—influencing the government to adopt policies they think are the correct ones, and in some cases, beneficial to them.

Nevertheless, since we have seen that these policies they advocate are not in our best interests, then we must oppose them and contest with them for the positions of power in our government.

I hardly need to mention that their money power vastly exceeds the money power available to us. They have used their money power cleverly—to influence elections, to influence decisions, to influence media, to influence universities. Since the days when Wall Street money quietly financed *The New Republic* to provide the left with an opportunity to blow off steam, these very smart people have recognized the importance of the media in directing people's attention toward certain issues and away from certain other issues.

Can this combination of money and media and political power be overcome? I think so. The alternative power source remaining to ordinary working men and women, to retirees, veterans and students is political. Not only can we vote, but we can run for office and campaign for people. But if this political power is to be used to its fullest potential, we must become far more sophisticated and knowledgeable than we have been in the past.

One of the ways our political power is diluted is by divisiveness. One old politician put it this way: "Every time the good folks get to fighting among themselves, the scalawags walk off with the election." He spoke the truth and surely some elements in this country have consciously sought to divide us for just that purpose.

Many politicians, for example, consistently stress differences rather than our common heritage. We are encouraged to categorize ourselves as male or female, black, white or ethnic, young or senior, labor or welfare, military or civilian, and Christian or Jew.

You can see where this leads if you think about it. Once we put ourselves in one of these categories and begin to think politically only about the narrow interests of that category, we fail to look at the larger picture and become an easy mark for the opportunistic politician.

In reality, we have far more in common than these categories indicate. First, we are all Americans no matter what our color, religion, ethnic background, sex, age, or occupation. We share a common heritage, a common land, a common enemy and in war, a common fate. We are all simultaneously both producers and consumers. We all desire fundamentally the same things: freedom, a decent job, enough income to provide a home, health care and education for our children, some independence when we retire. We all want an opportunity to love and to be loved and to be respected as individuals and treated with dignity. We all wish for peace in which to pursue these goals.

If we are to utilize the political power that is available to us, then we must resist efforts to divide us and concentrate on our common goals and shared characteristics. Above all, we must look beyond our narrow personal interests to our wider interests as American citizens. We must demand of all public officials, as a minimum, compliance with their oath of office and honesty and dedication. We must become sophisticated enough to become immune to manipulation by personal favor or the single issue.

We must realize that many public officials today are cynical and opportunistic and quick to exploit us to serve their own selfish purposes. I have seen veterans, for example, make their political judgments solely on the basis of a politician's attitude toward veterans' legislation. This is most common and you see the same thing happen with senior citizens, women in favor of or opposed to the ERA, union members, environmentalists, and so on down the list of "special interest" categories in which we put ourselves.

You see how vulnerable this makes us to manipulation. A politician might vote right on our special interests but be a disaster to the national interest.

Perhaps it would help if we could think of ourselves as two people whenever we approach a politician. One person is our smaller self. We might question a candidate on how he stands on issues that directly affect us. But then we must become a second person, our larger self, a personal representative of the United States of America. As a representative of our country, we would ask an entirely different set of questions.

You and I are indeed the personal representatives of America. We are the country. There is no one to defend our Constitution except us, the American people. There is no one who really cares if our nation survives, except us, the American people. The fate of our nation literally is in our hands. It has been entrusted to us by generations which have passed on.

Whether it remains a republic or becomes a dictatorship is our responsibility; whether America remains strong or grows weak is our responsibility. There is no "George" to do it—what is to be done must be done by us.

In fact, you and I must accept the responsibility for our present weakness, for the corruption in government, and for the blunders in foreign policy. We cannot escape responsibility because an elite began to play a dominant role in our government, for we allowed them to do it. We have always had the power to make changes; we have not always used that power.

In the last analysis we win or lose in peacetime as civilians just as we do in war on the battlefield. There is no way an officer can totally motivate his men to do their job in combat. He can train them in the skills they need, he can issue an order and he can set an example, but when it comes down to the moment of truth, each man must find within himself the will and the courage to do what is asked of him.

I think the future of our country boils down to this simple proposition: either we as individual Americans will assume the responsibilities of citizenship or our nation, as the land of the free, will be destroyed.

These responsibilities include developing a strong individual sense of nationalism while maintaining the individual liberty and entrepreneurial spirit that created and developed this great nation. They include exerting the energy necessary to become informed and knowledgeable, having the courage to stand up for our country and challenge misguided or ill-intentioned individuals, and making the political process work to produce the type of honest and courageous leaders we need.

We are living in a time of crisis, when the fate of our nation will be determined within a few short years. What will determine that fate will be fundamental decisions by individual Americans like you. If we decide to view ourselves only in terms of our own individuality, as persons whose welfare and fate are separate and distinct from the welfare and fate of the nation, then there is no hope for the survival of the United States. A wise enemy will always leave room for the individual to trade his nation's welfare for his own welfare—at least what he thinks is his own welfare.

The United States can only survive the coming crisis if enough of us choose to view ourselves as American nationalists, as a distinct people whose welfare and fate are married to those of the nation. Only as American nationalists will we view what is good for the nation as good for us and what is evil for the nation as evil for us. Without this marriage of individual and national interests, people simply will not exert the necessary energy to make the necessary sacrifices that will be required to preserve the Republic.

I will not mislead you. The preservation of the United States will not be an easy task. Shirkers and cowards and those grown too soft to endure conflict will hide. The influential will not relinquish their influence without a fight. The faint-hearted will wring their hands. You will have to suffer abuse and sharp debate and be prepared to hear a thousand "experts" call you wrong and a fool.

For what is necessary to preserve America is to go into the political arena with great determination and wrest, peacefully but firmly, the power from the hands of those who now have it. Only then can we set the United States back on a course of liberty and strength.

Those of you who have the grit and the courage to meet the challenge will be remembered by generations to come just as we today remember those who met the challenge of the American revolution.

I am confident we can succeed. I can already see a new America rising as from a sleep and shaking off the mistakes and blunders of the past four decades.

I can see an America in which the people once more walk with a firm step, their heads high, with quiet confidence and great pride.

I can see an America at work with its factories humming, with its cities rebuilt and its streets safe again for strolls on summer evenings . . . an America led by men and women of integrity and ability and courage . . . an America so strong and so bold that no enemy dare attack her, no mob dare touch her flag, no petty despot dare harm her citizens . . . an America that provides the world with a shining example and an eternal source of hope for those who love liberty and respect human rights.

Let us keep this vision clear in our hearts and then roll up our sleeves and go to work to make it a reality.